Dear Daddy John,

Hope you will find that little book interesting, especially nowadays when history seems to repeat itself.

Happy Birthday!

Love from

Elizabeth

THE ORDER OF THE DAY

ALSO BY ÉRIC VUILLARD

Sorrow of the Earth

ORDER

DAY

Éric Vuillard

Translated from the French by Mark Polizzotti

OTHER PRESS
NEW YORK

Production editor: Yvonne E. Cárdenas
Text designer: Jennifer Daddio / Bookmark Design & Media Inc.
This book was set in Centaur MT by
Alpha Design & Composition of Pittsfield, NH

3 5 7 9 10 8 6 4 2

Library of Congress Cataloging-in-Publication Control Number:
2018000872 (print)

For

LAURENT ÉVRARD

THE ORDER OF THE DAY

A SECRET MEETING

*T*he sun is a cold star. Its heart, spines of ice. Its light, unforgiving. In February, the trees are dead, the river petrified, as if the springs had stopped spewing water and the sea could swallow no more. Time stands still. In the morning, not a sound, not even birdsong. Then an automobile, and another, and suddenly footsteps, unseen silhouettes. The play is about to begin, but the curtain won't rise.

It's Monday. The city is just beginning to stir behind its scrim of fog. People go to work as on any other day; they board the bus or trolley, thread their way onto the upper deck, then daydream in the chill. And even though the twentieth of February 1933 was not just any other day, most people spent the morning grinding away, immersed in the great, decent fallacy of work, with its small gestures that enfold a silent, conventional truth and reduce the entire epic of our lives to a diligent pantomime. The day passed, quiet and normal. And while everyone shuttled between house and factory, market and courtyard where the laundry is hung out to dry, or in the evening between office and tavern, before finally heading home—far away, far from the decent labors, far from domestic life, on the banks of the Spree, some men got out of their cars in front of a palace. Through doors obsequiously held open, they stepped from their huge black sedans and paraded in single file, dwarfed by the heavy sandstone columns.

There were twenty-four of them, near the dead trees on the bank: twenty-four overcoats in black, brown, or amber; twenty-four pairs of wool-padded shoulders; twenty-four three-piece suits, and the same number of pleated trousers with wide cuffs. The shadows entered the large vestibule of the palace of the President of the Assembly—though before long, there would be no more assembly, no more president, and eventually no more parliament. Only a heap of smoking rubble.

For now, they doffed twenty-four felt hats and uncovered twenty-four bald pates or crowns of white hair. They shook hands solemnly before mounting the stage. The venerable patricians stood in the huge vestibule, exchanging casual, respectable banter, as if at the starchy opening of a garden party.

The twenty-four silhouettes conscientiously took a first stairway, then trudged up another flight, step after step, occasionally halting so as not to overtax their old hearts. They climbed, hands gripping the copper rail, eyes half-shut, without admiring the elegant banister or the vaulting, as if on a heap of invisible dead leaves. At the narrow entrance, they were ushered to the right; and there, after several paces over the checkered tiles, they scaled the thirty steps leading to the third floor. I don't know who was first in line, and ultimately it doesn't matter: all twenty-four had to do exactly the same thing, follow the same path, turn right around the stairwell, until finally, on their left, they entered the salon through the wide-open doors.

They say that literature gives you license. So I could, for instance, make them turn around the Penrose stairs in perpetuity, going neither up nor down, or both at the same time. And indeed, that's pretty much the sense we get from books. The time of words—compact or fluid, dense or impenetrable, stretched out, granular—halts movement and leaves us mesmerized. Our heroes are in the palace for all eternity, as if in an enchanted castle. They are thunderstruck from the outset, petrified, frozen. The doors are simultaneously open and shut, the fanlights worn, dangling, smashed, or repainted. The stairwell gleams, but it is empty; the chandelier sparkles, but it is dead. We are everywhere in time. And so, Albert Vögler climbed the steps to the first landing, and there he raised his hand to his detachable collar, sweating, dripping with perspiration, feeling slightly dizzy. Beneath the large gilded lantern that lit the flights of stairs, he straightened his vest, undid a button, loosened his collar. Perhaps Gustav Krupp paused on the landing as well, giving Albert a compassionate word, a small apothegm on old age—showed a little solidarity, in short. Then Gustav went on his way and Albert Vögler remained there a few moments longer, alone beneath the chandelier: a huge, gold-plated vegetable with an enormous ball of light in the center.

Finally, they entered the small salon. Wolf-Dietrich, private secretary to Carl von Siemens, dawdled for a moment near the French windows, letting his eyes linger on the thin coat of frost dusting the balcony. For a moment he escaped from the petty intrigues of this world, borne on cotton wool. And while the others chitchatted and puffed on their Montecristos, jabbering about the cream or taupe color of the wrappers and whether they liked their cigars smooth or spiced (though all of them were partial to fat ring gauges), absently squeezing the fine gold bands—while all of this was happening, Wolf-Dietrich stood daydreaming at the window, wavering with the bare branches and floating above the Spree.

A few steps away, admiring the delicate plaster figurines decorating the ceiling, Wilhelm von Opel raised and lowered his thick round glasses. His family was among those that had risen over the generations, going, through promotions and accumulations of estates and grandiose titles, from small landowners around the municipality of Braubach to magistrates, then burgomasters, until Adam Opel—issued from his mother's indecipherable entrails and schooled in the tricks of the locksmith's trade—designed a marvelous sewing machine that marked the true onset of their glory. In reality, Adam invented nothing. He got himself hired by a manufacturer, kept a low profile, then made a few improvements. He married Sophie Scheller, who brought with her a substantial dowry, and named his first sewing machine after her. At that point, production soared. It took only a few years for the sewing machine to realize its potential, enter the mainstream, become part of everyday life. Its true inventors had come along too early. Once the success of his sewing machines was a fait accompli, Adam Opel branched off into velocipedes. But one night, a strange voice slipped through the half-open door. His heart felt cold, so cold. It wasn't the sewing machine's actual inventors come to beg for royalties, or his workers demanding their share of the profits. It was God claiming his soul: he had to give it back.

But companies don't die like men. They are mystical bodies that never perish. The Opel brand continued selling bicycles, then automobiles. Already at its founder's death, the firm counted fifteen hundred employees, and it kept growing. A company is a person whose blood rushes to the head. We call these *legal entities*. Their lives last much longer than ours. And so, on this twentieth of February, as Wilhelm ruminated in the small salon of the palace of the President of the Reichstag, the Opel company was already an old lady. By now it was just an empire within another empire, bearing only a distant relation to Adam the patriarch's sewing machines. And though the Opel company was a very wealthy dowager, she was nonetheless so elderly that almost no one noticed her anymore; she had faded into the landscape. By now, the Opel company was older than many states, older than Lebanon, older than Germany itself, older than most African nations, older even than Bhutan, where the gods became lost in the clouds.

MASKS

O ne by one, then, we could approach all twenty-four of these gentlemen as they enter the palace, flit past their collar studs and the knots of their ties, lose ourselves an instant in the trim of their mustaches, zone out among the pinstripes of their jackets, plunge into their sad eyes. And there, deep inside that yellow, bristly arnica flower, we would always find the same little door; we would pull the bell cord and be transported back in time to witness the same string of underhanded maneuvers, marriages of convenience, double dealings—the tedious saga of their exploits.

By that February 20, Wilhelm *von* Opel, Adam's son, had brushed the motor grease from beneath his fingernails once and for all, put away his bike, left behind his sewing machine, and now sported a nobiliary particle that encapsulated his entire family history. From the height of his sixty-two years, he cleared his throat and glanced at his watch, then looked around him with pinched lips. Hjalmar Schacht had done his job well; he would soon be appointed Director of the Reichsbank and Minister of the Economy. Around the table were Gustav Krupp, Albert Vögler, Günther Quandt, Friedrich Flick, Ernst Tengelmann, Fritz Springorum, August Rosterg, Ernst Brandi, Karl Büren, Günther Heubel, Georg von Schnitzler, Hugo Stinnes Jr., Eduard Schulte, Ludwig von Winterfeld, Wolf-Dietrich von Witzleben, Wolfgang Reuter, August Diehn, Erich Fickler, Hans von Loewenstein zu Loewenstein, Ludwig Grauert, Kurt Schmitt, August von Finck, and Dr. Stein. We're at the nirvana of industry and finance. There they sat, silent, well-mannered, and a little numb from having waited for almost twenty minutes. The smoke from their stogies made their eyes water.

As if in meditation, several shadows paused at a mirror and straightened their ties, making themselves at home in the small salon. Somewhere, in one of his four volumes on architecture, Palladio rather nebulously defines a salon as a living room, the stage on which we play out the vaudeville of our existence. And in the celebrated Villa Godi Malinverni, starting from the Olympus Room, where nude gods cavort among the trompe l'oeil ruins, through the Room of Venus, where a child and a page escape through a painted false door, you arrive at the Main Hall, where you find, on an architrave above the entrance, the end of a prayer: "And deliver us from evil." But in the palace of the President of the Assembly, where our little gathering was being held, you would have searched in vain for such an inscription: it was not on the program. Not the order of the day.

A few more minutes dragged by beneath the tall ceiling. They exchanged smiles. They opened leather briefcases. Now and again, Schacht raised his gold-rimmed spectacles and rubbed his nose, tongue at the edge of his lips. The guests remained quietly seated, training their crab-like eyes on the door. Whispers between two sneezes. A handkerchief was unfolded, nostrils honked in the silence; then they shifted in their seats, waiting patiently for the meeting to begin. They were old hands at meetings. All of them sat on various boards of directors or of trustees; all were members of some employers' association or other. Not to mention the sinister family reunions of this austere and stultifying patriarchy.

In the front row, Gustav Krupp fanned his rubicund face with his glove, hawked conscientiously into his hanky: he had a cold. With age, his thin lips were beginning to form a nasty inverse crescent. He looked sad and worried. Mechanically he twisted a beautiful gold ring, through the fog of his hopes and calculations—and it's possible that, for him, those two words had but a single meaning, as if they'd been magnetically drawn together.

*S*uddenly, the doors creaked, the floorboards groaned; sounds of talking in the anteroom. The twenty-four lizards rose to their hind legs and stood stiffly. Hjalmar Schacht swallowed his saliva; Gustav adjusted his monocle. Behind the door panels, they heard muffled voices, then a whistle blast. And finally, the President of the Reichstag, Hermann Goering himself, strode smiling into the room. This was no surprise, really, just an everyday occurrence. In the grand scheme of business, partisan struggles didn't amount to much. Politicians and industrialists routinely dealt with each other.

Goering went around the table with a word for everyone present, seizing each hand in a debonair grip. But the President of the Reichstag had not come merely to welcome them. He mumbled a few words of greeting, then immediately launched into the upcoming elections, on March 5. The twenty-four sphinxes listened closely. The electoral campaign would be crucial, the President of the Reichstag announced. It was time to get rid of that wishy-washy regime once and for all. Economic activity demanded calm and stability. The twenty-four gentlemen nodded solemnly. The electric candles of the chandelier blinked; the great sun painted on the ceiling shone brighter than before. And if the Nazi Party won the majority, added Goering, these would be the last elections for ten years—even, he added with a laugh, for a hundred years.

A wave of approbation swept over the seats. At that moment, there was a sound of doors, and the new chancellor finally entered the room. Those who had never met him were curious to see him in person. Hitler was smiling, relaxed, not at all as they had imagined: affable, yes, even friendly, much friendlier than they would have thought. For everyone present, he had a word of thanks, a dynamic handshake. Once the introductions had been made, everyone again took their comfortable chairs. Krupp was in the first row, picking at his tiny mustache with a nervous finger. Right behind him, two directors of IG Farben, along with von Finck, Quandt, and some others, sagely crossed their legs. There was a cavernous cough. The cap of a pen produced a minuscule clink. Silence.

They listened. The basic idea was this: they had to put an end to a weak regime, ward off the Communist menace, eliminate trade unions, and allow every entrepreneur to be the führer of his own shop. The speech lasted half an hour. When Hitler had finished, Gustav stood up, took a step forward, and, on behalf of all those present, thanked him for having finally clarified the political situation. The chancellor made a quick lap around the table on his way out. They congratulated him courteously. The old industrialists seemed relieved. Once he had departed, Goering took the floor, energetically reformulating several ideas, then returned to the March 5 elections. This was a unique opportunity to break out of the impasse they were in. But to mount a successful campaign, they needed money; the Nazi Party didn't have a blessed cent and Election Day was fast approaching. At that moment, Hjalmar Schacht rose to his feet, smiled at the assembly, and called out, "And now, gentlemen, time to pony up!"

Cavalier though it was, the invitation was hardly novel to these men, who were used to kickbacks and backhanders. Corruption is an irreducible line item in the budget of large companies, and it goes by several names: lobbying fees, gifts, political contributions. Most of the guests immediately handed over hundreds of thousands of marks. Gustav Krupp gave a million, Georg von Schnitzler four hundred thousand, and so they raked in a hefty sum. That meeting of February 20, which might seem to us a unique moment in corporate history, an unprecedented compromise with the Nazis, was in fact nothing more for the Krupps, Opels, and Siemenses than a perfectly ordinary business transaction, your basic fund-raising. All would survive the regime and go on to finance many other parties, commensurate with their level of performance.

But to truly understand the meeting of February 20, 1933, to grasp its everlasting import, we must now call these men by their real names. It was not Günther Quandt, Wilhelm von Opel, Gustav Krupp, and August von Finck who were present that late afternoon, in the palace of the President of the Reichstag. We must use other designations. For "Günther Quandt" is a cryptonym; it masks something very different from the corpulent gentleman slicking down his mustache and sitting quietly in his seat around the table of honor. Close behind him is a rather more imposing silhouette, a tutelary shadow, as cold and impervious as a stone statue. Yes, hovering in all its fierce, anonymous power above Quandt and making him look stiff as a mask (but a mask that fits his face more closely than his own skin), we can see Accumulatoren-Fabrik AG, later called Varta—for as we know, legal entities have their avatars, just as ancient divinities took various forms and occasionally absorbed other divinities.

This, then, is the Quandts' real name, their demigod identity; whereas he, Günther, is but a tiny little mound of skin and bone like you and me. When he's gone, his sons will sit on the throne, then the sons of his sons. But the throne itself remains, even after the little mound of skin and bone has curdled in the earth. As such, these twenty-four men are not called Schnitzler, or Witzleben, or Schmitt, or Finck, or Rosterg, or Heubel, as their identity papers would have us believe. They are called BASF, Bayer, Agfa, Opel, IG Farben, Siemens, Allianz, Telefunken. By these names we shall know them. In fact, we know them very well. They are here beside us, among us. They are our cars, our washing machines, our household appliances, our clock radios, our homeowner's insurance, our watch batteries. They are here, there, and everywhere, in all sorts of guises. Our daily life is theirs. They care for us, clothe us, light our way, carry us over the world's highways, rock us to sleep.

And the twenty-four gentlemen present at the palace of the President of the Reichstag that February 20 are none other than their proxies, the clergy of major industry; they are the high priests of Ptah. And there they stand, affectless, like twenty-four calculating machines at the gates of Hell.

A COURTESY CALL

*A*n obscure inclination delivered us, passive and fearful, to the enemy. Ever since, the history books have not stopped rehashing the dread event, an unholy alliance of haste and reason. Once the high priests of industry and banking had been converted, then their opponents reduced to silence, the regime's only serious threat was from foreign powers. The situation with France and England grew tense, in a hodgepodge of power plays and conciliations. So it was that in November 1937, between two mood swings, and after several purely pro forma objections to the annexation of the Saarland, the remilitarization of the Rhineland, and the bombing of Guernica by the Condor Legion, Halifax, Lord President of the Council, went privately to Germany at the request of Hermann Goering, Reich Aviation Minister, Commander in Chief of the Luftwaffe, Reich Master of the Hunt and of the Forests, President of the defunct Reichstag, and creator of the Gestapo. That's a mouthful, yet Halifax did not bat an eyelid: the truculent, operatic figure, the notorious anti-Semite with his chestload of decorations, did not strike him as odd. Still, it's not as if Halifax was being gaslighted by someone who kept his cards close to the vest; not as if he failed to notice the dandified getups, the endless string of titles, the cryptic, delirious rants, the potbellied profile—hardly. A lot of water had gone under the bridge since the meeting of February 20, 1933, and by this point the Nazis had abandoned all self-restraint. The two men hunted together, dined together, shared a few laughs. And Hermann Goering, who lavished people with affection and friendship—he must have dreamed of being an actor, and in a way had become one—probably slapped old Halifax on the back, teased him a little, snowed him with a load of double-talk, the kind that leaves the interlocutor dazed and vaguely flustered, like an off-color joke.

We might say that the great huntsman enveloped Halifax in a scarf of fog and dust. And yet, Halifax, like the twenty-four high priests of German industry, must have been wise to Goering; he must have been familiar with his background, his career as a putsch-ist, his penchant for fanciful uniforms, his morphine addiction, his internment in Sweden, the crippling diagnoses of mental disorder, depression, and violent and suicidal tendencies. He must have seen right through the hero of early aviation, the World War I flying ace, the parachute merchant, the old veteran. Halifax was neither naïve nor an amateur. He must have been too well informed not to find their stroll together a bit peculiar, and at the end of that stroll we see the two men, in a brief film clip, admiring the bison preserve while a furiously relaxed Goering dispenses lessons on living well. He can't not have spotted the odd little feather in Goering's hatband, the fur collar, the eccentric tie. Maybe Halifax liked hunting, too, as his aged father did, and maybe he enjoyed his time in Schorfheide. But he can't have failed to notice Goering's strange leather jacket or the dagger in his belt, nor to pick up the sinister allusions couched in heavy-handed pleasantries. He might have seen him shooting arrows in some outlandish outfit; no doubt he saw the domesticated wild beasts, the lion cub that came to lick its master's face. And even if he saw none of that, even if he spent no more than a quarter of an hour with Goering, he surely heard about the vast circuit of model trains in his basement, and without a doubt he heard him spew a load of bizarre claptrap. And Halifax, the old fox, cannot have missed Goering's raving egomania. He might even have witnessed him suddenly letting go the wheel of his convertible and shouting into the wind! Yes, he must have divined the horrifying core beneath the pasty, bloated mask.

And then he met the Führer, and again Halifax didn't notice a thing. Ignoring Anthony Eden's reservations, he went so far as to intimate to Hitler that Germany's designs on Austria and part of Czechoslovakia did not seem unwarranted to His Majesty's government, as long as it all happened in a context of peaceful dialogue. He's not exactly a wild one, old Halifax. One final anecdote will give the measure of the man. In front of Berchtesgaden, where they let him off, Lord Halifax noticed a figure standing near the car, whom he took for a servant. He assumed the man had come to help him up the porch steps. And so, as they opened the door for him, he handed the fellow his overcoat. Immediately, von Neurath, or someone else, perhaps an actual footman, whispered hoarsely in his ear: "The Führer!" Lord Halifax raised his eyes. And it was indeed Hitler, whom he'd mistaken for a lackey! As he later recounted in his memoir, *Fullness of Days*, he simply hadn't bothered looking up: all he'd seen was a pair of trousers and two shoes. The tone is ironic: Lord Halifax is trying to make us laugh. But I don't think it's funny. The English aristocrat, the diplomat standing proudly behind his little line of forebears, deaf as trombones, dumb as buzzards, and blind as donkeys, leaves me cold. Wasn't it the Right Honourable first Viscount Halifax who, as Chancellor of the Exchequer, firmly opposed any special aid to Ireland throughout his term of office? The potato famine left a million dead. And the Right Honourable second viscount, Halifax's father, Groom of the King's Chamber, collector of ghost stories that one of his ghostly sons published after his death—is *he* someone to be proud of? And besides, that sort of tone-deafness is hardly unusual. These were not the foibles of a doddering old man, but the result of social blindness and arrogance. On the other hand, when it came to ideas, Halifax didn't mince words. About his conversation with Hitler, for instance, he would write to Baldwin: "Nationalism and Racialism is a powerful force but I can't feel that it's either unnatural or immoral!" And a short time later: "I cannot myself doubt that these fellows are genuine haters of Communism, etc.! And I daresay if we were in their position we might feel the same." Such were the foundations of what, still today, we call the Policy of Appeasement.

INTIMIDATIONS

*S*o we were talking about courtesy calls. And yet, on November 5, less than two weeks before Halifax came to talk peace with the Germans, Hitler had confided to his senior officers how he planned to occupy part of Europe by force. First they would invade Austria and Czechoslovakia. They were too cramped for space in Germany—and since no one is ever completely satisfied, and people are always turning toward hazy distant horizons, and a touch of megalomania overlaid with paranoid tendencies makes the slope even slipperier; and since, on top of that, they had already had the deliria of Herder and the addresses of Fichte, Hegel's "spirit of the people" and Schelling's dream of a communion of hearts, we can say that the notion of Lebensraum was really nothing new. Naturally, this meeting had remained secret, but we can guess what the atmosphere in Berlin must have been like just before Halifax's arrival. And that's not all. On November 8, nine days before his visit, Goebbels had inaugurated a huge art exhibition in Munich on the theme of "the eternal Jew." So much for maintaining the pretense. No one could have been unaware of the Nazis' plans, their brutal designs. The Reichstag Fire on February 27, 1933, the opening of Dachau that same year, the sterilization of the mentally ill that same year, the Night of the Long Knives the following year, the laws about blood purity and German honor, the inventory of racial characteristics in 1935: it was hard to miss.

In Austria, to which the Reich's ambitions immediately turned, Chancellor Dollfuss, who had arrogated full powers to himself—all four feet eleven inches of him—had been assassinated by Austrian Nazis in 1934. His successor, Kurt von Schuschnigg, had carried on his authoritarian policies. For several years, Germany had thus maintained a hypocritical diplomacy, a mishmash of assassinations, blackmail, and blandishments. Finally, barely three months after Halifax's visit, Hitler ratcheted things up. Schuschnigg, the little Austrian despot, was summoned to Bavaria. The day of clandestine maneuvers was over; the time for diktats had come.

*O*n February 12, 1938, Schuschnigg went to Berchtesgaden to meet with Adolf Hitler. He arrived at the station dressed up as a skier, the pretext for his trip being winter sports. And while they loaded his skiing equipment onto the train, the festival in Vienna was in full swing. For it was carnival time— and so the most joyous dates sometimes coincide with history's most sinister events. Fanfare, quadrille, the grand finale. They were playing one of Strauss's 150 waltzes, full of elegance and charm, beneath an avalanche of sweets. The carnival of Vienna is certainly less renowned than the ones in Venice and Rio. People don't wear such handsome masks or indulge in such frenetic dances. It's really nothing more than a string of galas. But even so, it's a big celebration. The constitutional bodies of the small, corporate Catholic state organize the merry-making. And so, as Austria was in its death throes, its chancellor, disguised as a ski buff, slipped away under cover of darkness on his improbable journey. And the Austrians kept on partying.

*I*n the morning, at Salzburg Station, there was just a cordon of gendarmes. The weather was chilly and damp. The car carrying Schuschnigg skirted the airfield, then took to the highway; the wide gray skies left him pensive. His reverie gave over to the rumbling of the car, the flecks of frost. Every life is miserable and solitary; every road is sad. The border lay just ahead, and Schuschnigg was suddenly seized by apprehension. He felt as if the truth was just beyond his grasp.

At the border, Franz von Papen had come to greet him. His long, elegant face reassured the chancellor. As they got into the car, von Papen mentioned casually that three of Germany's top generals would also be present at the meeting—"You don't mind, I hope?" Such obvious attempts at intimidation, such blunt maneuvers, often leave us speechless. We don't dare utter a word. Something deep within us, someone way too polite and timid, answers in our stead, says the opposite of what should be said. And so Schuschnigg did not protest and they started on their way, as if nothing had happened. As he stared dully at the road passing by, a troop carrier overtook his car, followed by two armored cars of the SS. The Austrian chancellor felt a muted anxiety. What was he doing in this hornet's nest? Slowly they climbed toward Berchtesgaden. Schuschnigg gazed at the tops of the pines, laboring to overcome his malaise. He kept silent. Von Papen also said nothing. Then the car arrived at the Berghof; the gate opened and shut. Schuschnigg had the awful feeling he'd fallen into a trap.

INTERVIEW
AT THE BERGHOF

*A*t around eleven in the morning, after several rounds of pleasantries, the doors to Adolf Hitler's study closed behind the Austrian chancellor. And then began one of the most fantastic and grotesque scenes of all time. We have only one person's testimony: that of Kurt von Schuschnigg himself.

It occurs in the most painful chapter of his memoir, *Austrian Requiem*. After a somewhat pedantic epigraph by Tasso, the narrative begins at one of the windows in the Berghof. The Austrian chancellor has just taken a seat at the Führer's invitation. He crosses and uncrosses his legs uncomfortably. He feels numb, sapped of strength. His earlier anxiety has returned, suspended from the coffered ceiling, lurking under the armchairs. Not quite knowing what to say, Schuschnigg looks away to admire the view; he enthusiastically mentions all the pivotal decisions that must have been made in this room. Immediately Hitler cuts him off: "We did not get together to speak of the fine view or of the weather!" Schuschnigg is staggered. Then he tries, with a stiff, awkward peroration, to regain his footing, bringing up the sorry Austro-German Agreement of 1936, as if he'd come here simply to address a few minor hiccups. Finally, in a last, desperate attempt, clinging to his good faith as if to a paltry life buoy, the Austrian chancellor states that these past years he has maintained German-friendly policies, strictly German-friendly policies! That's the opening Hitler has been waiting for.

"Ah! So you call this a friendly policy, Herr Schuschnigg? On the contrary, you have done everything to *avoid* a friendly policy!" he screams. And after another awkward attempt by Schuschnigg to justify himself, Hitler, in a rage, cranks it up a notch: "Besides, Austria has never done anything that would be of any help to Germany. The whole history of Austria is just one uninterrupted act of high treason."

Schuschnigg's palms are moist, and how large the room appears! And yet, on the surface, all is calm. The chairs are upholstered in vulgar fabric, the cushions are too soft, the woodwork plain, the lampshades fringed with little pompoms. Suddenly, Schuschnigg finds himself alone in the cold grass, under the vast winter sky, facing the mountains. The window grows beyond all proportion. Hitler glares at him with his pale eyes. Schuschnigg crosses his legs again and straightens his glasses.

For now, Hitler calls him "Mister Schuschnigg," while Schuschnigg continues to call him "Chancellor." Hitler has shut him down, and Schuschnigg, trying to make his case, has stressed his German-friendly policies. And now here the German chancellor is insulting Austria, even screaming that its entire contribution to German history is a big fat goose egg. And the tolerant, magnanimous Schuschnigg, instead of turning on his heels and ending the conversation then and there, furiously racks his brains, like a good pupil, for an example of Austria's famous contributions to history. At top speed, in no order whatsoever, he rummages through the pockets of the centuries. But his head is empty, the world is empty, Austria is empty. And the Führer's eyes stubbornly bore into him. So what does he finally come up with, in his desperate haste? Beethoven. He comes up with good old Ludwig, the irascible deaf composer, the republican, the hopeless hermit. It's Beethoven he drags out of the woodwork, swarthy Beethoven, the drunkard's son; he's the one that Kurt von Schuschnigg, the Austrian chancellor, the fearful little racist aristocrat, pulls from the pocket of History and dangles in Hitler's face like a white flag. Poor Schuschnigg. He tries to brandish a composer against raving delirium; he tries to brandish the Ninth Symphony against the threat of military aggression; he tries to brandish the three little notes of the *Appassionata* to prove that Austria did, too, play a role in history.

"Beethoven," Hitler retorts with an unexpected jab, "is not Austrian, he's German." And it's true. Schuschnigg hadn't even considered this. Beethoven is German, no two ways about it. Born in Bonn. And no matter how you slice it, even if you quietly try to stretch the truth a bit, even if you were to rifle through all the annals, Bonn has never been an Austrian city, never ever. Bonn is as far from Austria as Paris! You might as well claim that Beethoven was Romanian, or Ukrainian, since they're just as close. And why not Croatian while we're at it, or from Marseilles, since that's not much farther from Vienna?

"That's true," Schuschnigg stammers, "but he's Austrian by adoption." No doubt about it, this is not your typical summit meeting.

The weather was foul. The interview came to a close. They still had to lunch together. Side by side they walked downstairs. Before entering the dining room at the Berghof, Schuschnigg was struck by the portrait of Bismarck: the great chancellor's left eyelid drooped inexorably, his gaze was cold and disillusioned, his skin looked flaccid. They entered the room and sat down, Hitler at the middle of the table and the Austrian chancellor opposite. The meal progressed normally. Hitler was relaxed, even chatty.

In a childish outburst, he said that in Hamburg he was going to build *the largest bridge in the world*. And then, clearly unable to restrain himself, he added that soon he would put up *the tallest buildings*, and then the Americans would see that Germany built bigger and better houses than the United States. After that, they retired to the sitting room. Coffee was served by young members of the SS. Finally, Hitler took his leave, and the Austrian chancellor immediately began smoking like a chimney.

The photos we have of Schuschnigg show two different faces: one pinched and austere, the other shy, withdrawn, almost dreamy. In one famous picture, his lips are pressed together and he looks lost, his body in a posture of abandonment, as if falling. This was taken in his Geneva apartments in 1934. Schuschnigg is standing, perhaps worried. Something about his face looks spineless and indecisive. He appears to be holding a piece of paper in his hand, but the image is fuzzy and a dark stain obscures the bottom of the photo. If you look closely, you'll notice that the flap of one of his jacket pockets has been folded back by his arm, and then you spot a strange object, maybe a plant, intruding onto the scene from the right. But few people know this version of the photo. In order to see it, you have to go to the Bibliothèque Nationale de France, Prints and Photographs Department. The more familiar version has been cropped and reframed. Therefore, apart from a few assistant archivists in charge of cataloging and conserving documents, virtually no one has ever seen Schuschnigg's rumpled pocket flap, or the strange plant (or whatever it is) on the right-hand side, or the sheet of paper. Once reframed, the photo gives a wholly different impression. It takes on a kind of official significance, a certain decency. They only had to suppress a few meaningless millimeters, a tiny shard of truth, for the Austrian chancellor to seem more serious, less dim-witted than in the original shot—as if the simple fact of having tightened the crop a bit, erased a few disorderly elements, and refocused attention on himself conferred some density onto Schuschnigg. Such is the art of narrative: nothing is innocent.

But at that moment, at the Berghof, there was no question of density or decency. Here, there was only

one framing that counted, only one art of persuasion,
only one means of getting what you wanted: fear. In
this house, fear was what prevailed. No more allusive
niceties, subtle forms of authority, or maintaining a
friendly face. Here, the little Junker was quaking. First
of all, he, Schuschnigg, couldn't get over that someone
would dare speak to him that way. As he confided to
one of his aides soon afterward, he felt insulted. And
still, he didn't leave, didn't show any displeasure; he
just smoked. Butt after butt after butt.

Two long hours dragged by. Then, at around
4 p.m., Schuschnigg and his adviser were invited to
join Ribbentrop and von Papen in the next room.
They were presented with some clauses from a new
accord between their two countries, it being specified
that these were the Führer's final concessions. And
what did this accord require? For starters, in an empty,
fairly meaningless phrase, it required Austria and the
Reich to consult each other on international matters
that concerned both parties. It also required—and
here the plot thickened—that National-Socialist doctrine be permitted in Austria, and that Seyss-Inquart,

a Nazi, be named Minister of the Interior, with full powers over the police: a serious bit of interference. It further required that Dr. Fischböck, a notorious Nazi, be appointed to a cabinet post. Then it required amnesty for any Nazis in Austrian jails, including those convicted of felonies. It required that all National-Socialist civil servants and officers who had been relieved of their positions be fully reinstated. It demanded the immediate exchange of a hundred officers between the German and Austrian armies and the appointment of the Nazi Glaise-Horstenau as the Austrian Minister of War. Finally, it demanded—yet another affront—the dismissal of the Austrian propaganda directors. These measures to go into effect in one week, in return for which—a superb concession—"the German Reich Government reaffirms the agreements of July 11, 1936," which had just been hollowed out, and "renews its full recognition of Austria's sovereignty and independence." And after all the above, one final, astounding flourish: Germany "specifically abstains from any intervention in Austria's interior political affairs." Unreal.

Then the discussions started, and Schuschnigg tried to lower the Germans' demands; but more than anything, he tried to save face. They haggled over a few details, like frogs competing for the same pond. Finally, Ribbentrop agreed to amend three clauses, and after more laborious negotiations he made a few trifling revisions. The talks came to a sudden halt when Hitler summoned Schuschnigg.

*T*he office is bathed in lamplight. Hitler strides across it. Once more, the Austrian chancellor feels uneasy. And the moment he sits down, Hitler goes on the attack, announcing that he will consent to one final attempt at reconciliation. "Here is the draft of the document," he says. "There is nothing to be discussed about it. I will not change one single iota. You will either sign it as it stands or else our meeting has been useless. In that case I shall decide during the night what will be done next." The Führer has never looked more serious or more sinister.

———

*N*ow Schuschnigg was facing his moment of grace or disgrace. Would he cave in to these bush-league machinations and accept the ultimatum? The body is an instrument of pleasure. Adolf Hitler's bustles about wildly. He is stiff as an automaton and virulent as a gob of phlegm. Hitler's body has evidently penetrated our dreams and consciousness; we seem to find him in the shadows of time, on the walls of prisons, crawling under trestle beds, wherever men have sketched the figures that haunt them. So it's possible that, at the very moment when Hitler was throwing his ultimatum at Schuschnigg's head, just when the fate of the world, via the capricious coordinates of time and space, found itself for a fleeting instant in Kurt von Schuschnigg's hands, it's possible that several hundred miles away, in his asylum in Ballaigues, Louis Soutter was sketching one of his obscure dances on a paper napkin with his fingers. Hideous, terrible puppets skitter on the horizon, over which rolls a black sun. They flee in every direction, skeletons, ghosts, surging from the fog. Poor Soutter. He had already spent fifteen years in the asylum, fifteen years painting his anguish on ratty bits of paper, used envelopes that he fished from the wastebasket. And his obscure little figures, twisted like wire, created just as the fate of Europe was being decided in the Berghof, strike me as omens.

Soutter had returned from an extended stay abroad, far, far away from home, at the other end of the world, in a worrisome state of collapse. After which, he had gotten by as best he could. A violinist at tea dances during the tourist season, he was dogged wherever he went by a reputation as a kook. His face took on a deep melancholy. And he was institutionalized in the Jura Asylum in Ballaigues. Sometimes he ran away, and they would bring him back, mere skin and bones, half-dead from the cold. Upstairs, in his room, he piled up drawing after drawing, a monstrous heap of sketches, depicting deformed black creatures, great palpitating invalids. His own body was so skinny, so worn out by long rambles in the wild. His cheeks were cavernous and he had lost all his teeth. The arthritis in his hands made it impossible for him to hold a brush or pen, and around 1937, nearly blind, he began painting with his fingers, dipping them directly in the ink. He was almost seventy by then. And that's when he created his most sublime works: hordes of black, agitated, frenetic silhouettes. They looked like clusters of blood, or grasshoppers in flight. And that frenzied agitation lived in Louis Soutter's mind like an obsessive terror. But given what was happening in Europe during those long years of reclusion in Ballaigues, we could say that his string of dark, twisted, suffering, gesticulating bodies, those necklaces of corpses, were heralds. We could say that poor Soutter, imprisoned in his delirium, might unwittingly have captured the slow death agony of the world around him. We could say that old Soutter made the whole world parade by, the specters of the whole world, behind a paltry hearse. Everything became flame and thick smoke. He dipped his misshapen fingers into the small ink bottle and delivered the moribund truth of his times: one big danse macabre.

At the Berghof, they were far from Louis Soutter, his strange timidity, and the dining hall in Ballaigues. They were engaged in more sordid affairs. While Louis Soutter was perhaps sticking his arthritic finger in his bottle of black ink, Schuschnigg was staring fixedly at Adolf Hitler. He would later write in his memoirs that Hitler exerted a magical influence over people. And he added, "The Führer drew others to him by magnetic force, then pushed them away with such violence that an abyss opened, which nothing could fill." Schuschnigg didn't stint on esoteric rationales. It justified his weakness. The Reich Chancellor was a supernatural being, the one that Goebbels's propaganda machine wanted us to see, a fantastic creature, fearsome and inspired.

*A*nd in the end, Schuschnigg gave in. Worse, he equivocated. He said he was ready to sign but he mumbled one last objection, the most timid, irresolute, and craven of all: "I want to make it quite clear," he added, in a perceptible mix of spite and weakness that must have contorted his features, "that my signature alone can be of no value whatsoever to you." At that moment, he must have savored Hitler's look of surprise. He must have savored the one small spark of superiority over Adolf Hitler that he was able to snatch from fate. Yes, he must have reveled in that feeble gesture. The silence that followed his retort lasted an eternity. Schuschnigg felt invincible and puny. And he squirmed in his seat.

Hitler looked stunned. What was this man telling him? "According to our constitution," Schuschnigg went on in professorial tones, "Cabinet members are appointed by the head of the State, the President, just as it is only the President who can grant an amnesty." So that was it: he wasn't content merely with giving in to Adolf Hitler; he also had to hide behind someone else. Suddenly, when his power became a poisoned chalice, the little autocrat agreed to share it.

But the strangest part was the reaction of Hitler, who stammered back, "So, you have the right..." as if he couldn't quite grasp what was happening. Objections of constitutional law were beyond him.

The man who, for the sake of his propaganda, did all he could to keep up appearances, must suddenly have felt disoriented. Constitutional law is like math, you can't cheat. He stammered again, "You have to..." And Schuschnigg must really have been relishing his triumph—he'd got him at last! With his law, he'd got him; with his law studies and his degree! The brilliant attorney had snared the ignorant little agitator. Yes, constitutional law exists, and it's not for mice or termites, but for chancellors, true statesmen. For a constitutional regulation, sir, can block your path just as effectively as a tree trunk or police barricade!

That's when Hitler, in high dudgeon, yanked open his office door and yelled into the vestibule, "General Keitel!" Then, turning back to Schuschnigg, he hissed, "I shall have you called later." Schuschnigg left, and the door closed.

At the Nuremberg Trials, General Keitel related the scene that followed. He was the sole remaining witness. When the general walked into the Führer's office, Hitler simply asked him to be seated, then sat down in turn. Behind the mysterious wooden doors, the Führer declared that he had nothing in particular to say to Keitel, then sat still and quiet for a moment. No one moved. Hitler was absorbed in thought and Keitel sat beside him, saying nothing. The chancellor, in fact, saw Keitel as a pawn, a mere pawn, nothing more, and was using him as such. That's why, strange as it might seem, over the long minutes of their consultation, nothing happened. Absolutely nothing. At least, that's Keitel's story.

During this time, Schuschnigg and his adviser feared the worst, including their arrest. Forty-five minutes went by... With Ribbentrop and von Papen, they continued mechanically to discuss the clauses of the accord. But what was the point, since Hitler had already stated he wouldn't change an iota? It must have been Schuschnigg's way of reassuring himself; at all costs, the situation had to appear entirely normal. And so he continued to act as if this were really a summit meeting between heads of state, and he still the representative of a sovereign nation. But in reality, he was only trying to avoid making his painful situation look official, and therefore irremediable.

$\mathcal{F}$inally, Hitler called Kurt von Schuschnigg back in. And then—the mysteries of charisma, when one blows first cold and then hot, when the tone changes from one act to the next—the thorns suddenly disappeared. "I have decided to change my mind—for the first time in my entire life," Adolf Hitler announced, as if granting a magnanimous favor. At that instant, Hitler might have smiled. When gangsters or lunatics smile, they are hard to resist; best to get it over with quickly and restore peace. And besides, between two bouts of emotional torture, a smile no doubt possesses a special charm, like a clearing sky. "But I warn you," Hitler added, mixing gravity with confidence, "this is your very last chance. I have given you three more days before the agreement goes into effect." At which point, even though nothing had changed, though the minuscule amendments he'd negotiated had just gone out the window and the time limit had been cut by more than half, Schuschnigg accepted without turning a hair. Worn down, as if he had gained some major concession, he got behind an agreement that was even more calamitous than the first.

Once the documents had been sent to the secretaries' office, the conversation resumed on a friendlier note. Hitler now called Schuschnigg "Mister Chancellor," which took the cake. Finally, everyone signed the typewritten copies, and the Reich Chancellor proposed that Schuschnigg and his adviser stay for dinner. They politely declined the invitation.

THE ART OF INDECISION

*I*n the days that followed, the German army indulged in intimidation tactics. Hitler had asked his best generals to simulate preparations for an invasion. The extraordinary thing is that, while we have seen all kinds of feints throughout military history, this one was different. It wasn't a piece of strategy or maneuvering, since no one was at war. It was simply a psychological ploy, a threat. It's hard to imagine German generals lending themselves to this make-believe offensive. They must have gunned the engines, spun the propellers, and, with a smirk, let their troop carriers idle at the border.

In Vienna, in the office of President Miklas, panic was rising: ploys can be effective. The Austrian government imagined the Germans were indeed getting ready to invade. And so they dreamed up all sorts of follies. They figured they could appease Hitler by making him a gift of his native town, Braunau am Inn, with its ten thousand inhabitants, its Fischbrunnen fountain, its hospital, its taverns. Yes, let's give him back his hometown, the house where he was born, with its lovely scalloped fanlights. Let's give him this scrap of his childhood and maybe he'll leave us alone! Schuschnigg, desperate to hold on to his little throne, didn't know what to think up next. Fearing an imminent German attack, he begged Miklas to endorse the agreement and appoint Seyss-Inquart as Minister of the Interior. Seyss-Inquart is not a monster, Schuschnigg wheedled, he's a *moderate* Nazi, really just a patriot. And besides, this keeps everything among the right sort of people—for Seyss-Inquart the Nazi and Schuschnigg the little dictator whom Hitler tyrannized were practically friends. They had both studied law, skimmed through Justinian's *Institutes*. They had both published papers: one, a short scholarly note on masterless slaves, a mysterious concept handed down from Roman jurisprudence; the other, a much-discussed report on some controversial point or other of canon law.

On top of which, both were crazy about music. They especially admired Bruckner, and together they sometimes chatted about his musical vocabulary, in the Chancellery offices where the Congress of Vienna had taken place, in the corridors that had witnessed Talleyrand's sharp-toed boots and sharper tongue. Schuschnigg and Seyss-Inquart talked of Anton Bruckner in the shadow of Metternich, that other specialist of peace; they talked of Bruckner's life of piety and modesty. At those words, Schuschnigg's glasses fogged up and his voice grew husky. Perhaps he was thinking of his first wife, the horrible car accident, the years of remorse and sorrow. Seyss-Inquart raised his little scarab-like glasses and mulled over long sentences, near the corridor windows. He whispered, moved, that Bruckner—the poor man—had been interned, for three months. Schuschnigg looked down. And Seyss-Inquart, pensive, a vein throbbing on his forehead, said that Anton Bruckner, during his very long and monotonous strolls, would count the leaves on the trees; that with a kind of secret, sterile obstinacy he went from tree to tree, watching in tormented anxiety as their numbers grew. He also kept count of cobble-stones, of windows on houses, and when he chatted with a woman, he couldn't help making a quick mental count of the pearls on her necklace. He counted the hairs on his dog, the hairs on passersby, the clouds in the sky. They labeled this an obsessive-compulsive neurosis; it was like a fire consuming him. As such, added Seyss-Inquart, staring at the chandeliers in the grand hall, Bruckner separated his musical themes with mocking silences. Apparently, his symphonies were even based on a very subtle organizing principle, a regular succession of themes. In them, murmured Seyss-Inquart, letting his hand glide along the banister of the grand stairway, we find particular progressions obeying a logical foundation that is so strict, so implacable, that it was impossible for him to finish his Ninth Symphony. He had to stop working on the last movement for two years; and in some cases, his constant revisions left behind up to seventeen versions of a single passage.

Schuschnigg must have been fascinated by this deranged system, all hesitations and reversals. This

might have been why he and Seyss-Inquart especially loved—as a witness at the time has related—
conversing about Bruckner's Ninth Symphony, with its
grandiose brass, its harrowing pause, then the whisper
of a clarinet, and the moment when the violins slowly
spit their little stars of blood. Then they evoked the
conductor Furtwängler, his tall forehead, his gentle
bearing, and that baton that he held like a twig. Finally,
they came to Arthur Nikisch. And via Nikisch, who
performed Beethoven under the direction of Richard
Wagner; via Nikisch's simple beat that could bring
out the full sonority of the orchestra, as if those small,
sovereign movements could liberate the essence of the
work from the ink marks on the score; via Nikisch,
who was directed by Liszt, himself a student of Salieri,
providence gave them Beethoven and Mozart. And at
the far end of their rapture they encountered Haydn,
and stone-cold poverty. For Haydn, well before becoming the tireless and celebrated composer of operas,
symphonies, masses, oratorios, concertos, marches,
and dances, was the poor son of a wheelwright and a
cook, a miserable vagabond on the streets of Vienna,

who scraped by as a performer at funerals and weddings. But such struggles were not Schuschnigg and Seyss-Inquart's bailiwick. No, they'd rather branch off onto a different path, and traipse with Liszt through the tony salons of Europe.

For Seyss-Inquart, however, the stroll would end much worse than for Schuschnigg: after holding offices in Krakow and The Hague, he finished his pathetic career as a walk-on at Nuremberg. And there, of course, he denied everything. The man who played a major part in Austria's incorporation into the Third Reich, had done nothing; who was awarded the honorary SS rank of *Gruppenfuhrer*, had seen nothing; who was minister without portfolio in Hitler's government, had heard nothing; who represented the Governor General of Poland and was implicated in the brutal putdown of the Polish resistance, had ordered nothing; the man who ultimately became *Reichskommissar* for the Netherlands and according to the Nuremberg indictments had more than four thousand people executed, who as a zealous anti-Semite eliminated Jews from every position of responsibility, who helped craft the policies that entailed the deaths of a hundred thousand Dutch Jews—this man knew nothing. And while the trumpets of Judgment sounded, for him this time, he dredged up his legal training, pled his case, referred to document after document, painstakingly shuffling through reams of evidence.

On October 16, 1946, at the age of fifty-four, the son of the school principal Emíl Zajtich (who had swapped the family name for something more Germanic), having spent his early childhood in Stannern in Moravia and moved to Vienna at the age of nine, found himself standing above the void in Nuremberg. And there, on the scaffold, after weeks in a cell, watched day and night under lamplight as blinding as an icy sun; after he'd been informed the night before that his final hour had come; after he'd descended the several steps to the courtyard and advanced shakily between rows of soldiers, then been the last to mount the scaffold; after the other nine convicts were dead, now it was his turn to stumble as he walked the line. In the makeshift structure where the gallows had been set up, which looked like a rickety fairground stall, Ribbentrop had been the first to go. Not arrogant, as he so often was, nor inflexible, as during the negotiations at the Berghof, but overwhelmed by his approaching death. A limping old man.

After Ribbentrop went the eight others, until it was time for him, Arthur Seyss-Inquart. He took a step toward the hangman, John C. Woods, his last witness. And beneath the floodlights, Seyss-Inquart, like a dazed butterfly, caught sight of Woods's beefy face. A medical evaluation, full of clumsy and self-contradictory jargon, states that Woods was mentally deficient—but who else could stand to do a job like that? Other witnesses have spoken of a pathetic loser, a boastful drunkard. They say that toward the end of his career as an executioner, after fifteen years of loyal service and with a dozen whiskeys in him, he would brag of having hanged 347 convicts, though this number has been contested. Whatever the case, by that day in October, he had already dispatched quite a few from this world since his modest beginnings; and

a photo shows him on another day in 1946, when with
the help of Johann Reichhart, a fellow hood-and-rope
man, he went about executing some thirty convicts:
the left-hand row for Woods, the right-hand one for
Reichhart, who for his part had already killed thousands for the Third Reich, and whom the Americans
had recruited for the cause. It was that ruddy round
face—for in the final account, death makes do with
what it has—that would usher Seyss-Inquart into the
Beyond.

Then Seyss-Inquart tried to find the words, but
where had they gone? Once you cleared away the salon
chitchat, the orders, and the courtroom debates, only
one sentence remained. A meaningless sentence. Words
so flimsy that the light showed through them, ending
in a strange shout: "I believe in Germany!" And Woods
finally placed the hood over his head and slipped the
rope around his neck, before activating the trapdoor.
And Seyss-Inquart, in the midst of a world in ruins,
abruptly disappeared down the hole.

A DESPERATE ATTEMPT

*B*ut we're still only on February 16, 1938. Several hours before the ultimatum expired, Miklas, cloistered in his presidential palace, also gave in. They pardoned Dollfuss's killers, Seyss-Inquart was named Minister of the Interior, and the SA paraded down the streets of Linz waving huge banners. On paper, Austria was dead; it had come under German supervision. But as we've seen, none of this has the density of nightmares or the grandiosity of terror; only the viscous clamminess of schemes and deception. No violent highs; no horrible, inhuman words: nothing more than blunt threats, and crude, repetitious propaganda.

And yet, a few days later, Schuschnigg suddenly got his back up. This forced agreement had stuck in his craw. In a final outburst, he declared in Parliament that Austria would remain independent and would go thus far and no further. The situation escalated. Members of the Nazi Party took to the streets and wreaked havoc. The police didn't lift a finger, since the Nazi Seyss-Inquart was already Minister of the Interior.

There's nothing worse than resentful masses, militias with their armbands and faux-military insignias, young people caught up in false dilemmas, squandering their passions on awful causes. At that moment, Schuschnigg, the little Austrian dictator, played his final card. Still, he must have known that, in any game, there comes a tipping point, after which it's hopeless. All you can do is watch your opponent lay down hand after winning hand and take every trick: queens, kings, all the cards you couldn't play in time and that you desperately held back, trying not to forfeit them. For Schuschnigg is nothing. He contributes nothing, is friend to nothing, is the hope of nothing. He's got nothing but flaws: aristocratic arrogance and reactionary political views. A man who, eight years earlier, established a paramilitary group of young Catholics. No shaft of daylight will slice through his dark night; no smile will break out on the specter's face and encourage him to carry out his final duty. His mouth will utter no lapidary words, no morsel of grace, no splutter of enlightenment. His face will not be bathed in tears. Schuschnigg is just a gambler, a paltry schemer. He even seems to have believed in the sincerity of his German neighbor, the integrity of the accords, even though they'd been extorted from him. It's a bit late in the day for alarm! He calls upon the goddesses he scorned, demands ridiculous commitments for an independence that is already dead—but he who dances on freedom's grave shouldn't expect it to come rushing to his aid. He has not wanted to look truth in the eye, and now here it is, up close, horrid, and inevitable. And it spits the doleful secret of his compromises right in his face.

And so, in a drowning man's last gasp, he tried to drum up support from the trade unions and Social Democrats, even though they'd been banned for the past four years. Realizing the danger, the socialists nonetheless agreed to back him. Schuschnigg immediately ordered a plebiscite on his country's independence. Hitler was livid.

On Friday, March 11, at five in the morning, Schuschnigg's valet woke him for the longest day of his existence. He lowered his feet from the bed. The parquet floor was cold. He put on his slippers. They told him of massive movements of German troops. The border at Salzburg was closed and railway traffic between Germany and Austria had been suspended. There was a snake in the grass. The burden of living was unbearable. He suddenly felt terribly, horribly old. But he'd have plenty of time to think about that, as he would spend seven years in prison under the Third Reich. He'd have seven years to ponder whether it had been the right thing to do back then, organizing his little paramilitary Catholic group; seven years to decide what is truly Catholic and what isn't, to separate the light from the ash. Even with privileges, incarceration is an ordeal. And so, once liberated by the Allies, he would finally lead a pacific life. And—as if it were possible for each of us to have two lives, as if the game of death could wipe our thoughts clean, as if in the darkness of those seven years he had called out to God, "Who am I?" and God had answered,

"Somebody else"—the former chancellor would settle in the United States and become a model American, a model Catholic, a model professor at the very Catholic Saint Louis University. We can almost imagine him sitting around in his dressing gown, chatting about the Gutenberg galaxy with Marshall McLuhan!

A DAY ON THE PHONE

At around ten that morning, while Albert Lebrun, President of the French Republic, signed a decree granting coveted *appellation contrôlée* status to Juliénas cru Beaujolais (Decree of March 11, 1938), and wondered, as his gaze tumbled down the shutters of his office window, whether the wines of Emeringes and Pruzilly also deserved that designation; while it rained outside and droplets struck the panes like a piano sonata played by an inexpert hand (thought Lebrun in a burst of lyricism); while he tossed the decree onto an enormous pile—what a mess!— and snatched up another, setting the budget for the National Lottery for the next accounting period (this had to be the fifth or sixth of those he'd signed since taking office, for certain decrees kept coming back, like swifts in the tall trees along the quays, to land on his desk year after year); while Albert Lebrun, then,

daydreamed behind the bourgeois vanity of his enormous lampshade, elsewhere, in Vienna, Chancellor
Schuschnigg received an ultimatum from Adolf Hitler:
either he rescinded his plebiscite, or Germany would
invade Austria. Nonnegotiable. No more virtuous fan-
tasies. Time to wipe off the makeup and remove the
costume. Four interminable hours passed. At 2 p.m.,
having blown off his lunch, Schuschnigg finally can-
celed the plebiscite. Whew. Everything could go on
just as before: strolls along the Danube, classical music,
empty prattling, pastries from Demel or Sacher…

Not so fast. The monster proved greedier still.
It now demanded Schuschnigg's resignation and his
replacement by Seyss-Inquart as Austrian chancellor.
Nothing less. "What a nightmare! Will it never end!"
Back when he was prisoner of the Italians, as a young
man in the First World War, Schuschnigg should have
read Gramsci instead of love stories—in which case,
he might have come across the line: "When debating
with an opponent, try to put yourself in his shoes." But
he had never put himself in anyone's shoes; at most, he
had tried on Dollfuss's suit, after several years spent

licking his boots. Put himself in someone else's shoes? He had no idea what that meant. He'd never gotten into the shoes of the battered workers, or the jailed trade unionists, or the tortured democrats; so the last thing we needed now was for him to get into the shoes of monsters! He hesitated. It was the very last minute of his very last hour. And then, as always, he capitulated. He, the man of power and religion, of order and authority, said yes to whatever they demanded. You just have to *not* ask nicely. He said no, firmly, to the freedom of the Social Democrats. He said no, courageously, to freedom of the press. He said no to the maintenance of an elected parliament. He said no to the right to strike, no to assemblies, no to the existence of parties other than his own. And this was the same man who would be hired after the war by the noble university of Saint Louis, Missouri, as a professor of political science. It's true he was well versed in political science, he who had managed to say no to every public freedom. And so, once his little moment of hesitation had passed, as a Nazi mob forced its way into the Chancellery, Schuschnigg the intransigent,

Mister No, negation made dictator, turned toward Germany and, with a strangled voice, red snout, and moist eye, uttered a feeble "yes."

There was really nothing else he could have done, he tells us in his memoirs. One takes what consolation one can. He thus set out for the presidential palace, relieved to the depths of his soul—bruised, but relieved. He would hand in his resignation to the President of the Republic, Wilhelm Miklas. But, surprise! Miklas, son of a minor postal worker, whom they'd kept on as president merely for show, who served as moral sanction and normally was content to stand quietly at ceremonies beside Dollfuss, then beside Schuschnigg—that nitwit Miklas refused to accept his resignation. Shit! They called up Goering. Goering had had it up to here with those stupid Austrians. Why couldn't they just leave him the hell alone, already! But Hitler saw things differently. Miklas had *better* accept that resignation, he screeched, a telephone receiver in each hand. That's an order! It's strange how the most dyed-in-the-wool tyrants still vaguely respect due process, as if they want to make it appear that they aren't abusing procedure, even while riding roughshod over every convention. It's as if power isn't enough for them, and that they take special pleasure in forcing their enemies to perform, one last time and for their benefit, the same rituals that they are even then demolishing.

A long day, that March 11! Tick tock, tick tock, the hands of the clock above Miklas's desk calmly made inching progress, like woodworms. Miklas was not what you'd call an outstanding leader. He'd let Dollfuss install his dictatorship in Austria, and by not making a peep had been allowed to retain his measly title as president. Word was that, in private, he voiced criticisms about such violations of the constitution. Big deal. And yet this Miklas was a curious fellow, because at the worst possible moment, at around two in the afternoon on March 11, when everyone was gripped by holy terror and Schuschnigg was repeating yes, yes, yes at the drop of a hat, suddenly Miklas was saying no. And he wasn't saying no to three unionists, two newspaper magnates, or a skinny bunch of Social Democrat deputies; he was saying no to *Adolf*

Hitler. Go figure. Dreary little Miklas, a simple figure-head, president of a republic that had been defunct for five years, was suddenly fighting back. With his big middle-manager's mug, his cane, three-piece suits, bowler hat, and watch fob, he no longer knew how to say yes. Man is never a sure bet; a poor bastard can suddenly dig way down deep inside himself and find an absurd scrap of resistance, a tiny nail, a splinter. And so it was that a man apparently without convictions, a nincompoop with little self-esteem, dug in his heels. Not for long, mind you, but even so. Miklas's day was far from over.

In the first instance, after hours of pressure, he had caved. The Nazis were relieved: though their tanks rolled on red carpets, they were anxious for Miklas's consent. "Yes, Schuschnigg can resign, fine, I've made up my mind about that." A strange concession—especially since, having agreed at seven-thirty to toss Schuschnigg into the dustbin of history, and while the reassured Nazis were chilling the champagne to toast Seyss-Inquart's enthronement, at seven-thirty-one old Miklas tugged on their sleeve to say that, while he accepted the resignation of that pinhead Schuschnigg, he categorically refused to appoint Seyss-Inquart.

By now it was past eight o'clock. And so, tired of threatening Miklas, the Germans—who, the history books tell us, cared hugely about keeping up appearances so as not to alarm the international community (which naturally suspected nothing)—decided to try a different tack. Never mind that Seyss-Inquart wasn't chancellor yet; they would call upon his services as Minister of the Interior. In order to send the Wehrmacht across the Austrian border without seeming to trample the rule of law, they asked Seyss-Inquart if he would be so kind as to officially invite the Germans to his lovely country, and be quick about it. True, he was only a minister, but since President Miklas didn't want to make him chancellor, they'd have to manhandle protocol a bit. One might be a stickler for the Constitution, but an urgent situation is an urgent situation.

And so they awaited Seyss-Inquart's call, the little telegram by which he'd ask the Nazis to come lend him a hand. Eight-thirty, and nothing had happened. The bubbly was going flat. What the hell was that

Seyss-Inquart doing? They were hoping it would all go quickly, that he'd hurry up and send his stupid telegram so they could finally go to dinner. Hitler was beside himself. He'd been waiting for hours! For years, in fact! And so, at his wits' end, at exactly eight-forty-five he gave the order to invade Austria. Too bad for Seyss-Inquart's appeal. They'd do without it! Too bad for rights, charters, constitutions, and treaties. Too bad for laws, those normative little abstract vermin, general and impersonal, Hammurabi's concubines, who supposedly treat everyone the same, the harlots! Isn't a fait accompli the surest of laws? They were going to invade Austria without anyone's permission, and they'd do it out of love.

Nonetheless, once the invasion was launched, they agreed that, all things considered, a proper invitation would put them on more solid ground. So they composed a telegram, the one they would have liked to receive: in matters of love, some are satisfied with dictating to their mistress the billets doux they dream of getting from her. Three minutes later, Seyss-Inquart received the text of the telegram that he was supposed to send Adolf Hitler—thereby transmuting the invasion, by a subtle retroactive effect, into an invitation. Bread becomes flesh, wine becomes blood. But it so happened—another surprise!—that the very obliging Seyss-Inquart did not feel entirely ready to sell Austria out. The minutes ticked by, and still the telegram didn't arrive.

Finally, at around midnight, at the end of an endless debate, when the Nazis had already seized the main centers of power; while Seyss-Inquart obstinately refused to sign his telegram; while the city of Vienna witnessed scenes of murderous insanity: riots, arson, screaming, Jews dragged by the hair through streets littered with rubble; while the great democracies took no notice, with England snoring peacefully, France dreaming sweet dreams, and no one giving a tinker's damn—while all this was happening, old Miklas, shrugging his heavy shoulders, exhausted and no doubt disgusted, grudgingly named the Nazi Seyss-Inquart Chancellor of Austria. Great catastrophes often creep up on us in tiny steps.

FAREWELL LUNCHEON
ON DOWNING STREET

*T*he following day, in London, Ribbentrop was invited by Chamberlain for a farewell luncheon. After several years in England, the Reich's ambassador had just received a promotion: henceforth, he would be Foreign Minister. He was back in London for a few days to say his farewells and return the house keys—for before the war, Chamberlain, who owned several properties, apparently counted Ribbentrop among his tenants. From this anodyne fact, this strange conflict between the image and the man, this contract by which Neville Chamberlain, the "lessor," agreed for a price, the "rent," to allow Joachim von Ribbentrop quiet enjoyment of his house in Eaton Square, no one has drawn the slightest inference. Chamberlain must have received his rent check between two pieces of bad news, two low blows. But business is business. No one, then, has detected any anomaly here, or conferred on this little morsel of Roman law the slightest significance. Some poor devil on trial for robbery gets slammed with a long list of priors, and suddenly the facts speak for themselves. But if those facts concern Chamberlain, well, it's steady on, old boy. A certain decency is called for. His politics of appeasement are just an unfortunate mistake, and his activities as a landlord are, in the annals of history, no more than a minor footnote.

The first part of the meal was perfectly pleasant and good-humored. Ribbentrop told stories of his athletic prowess, then, after a few jokes at his own expense, he brought up the pleasures of tennis; Sir Alexander Cadogan listened politely. Ribbentrop rambled on for a while about serves, and about that little globe of felt-covered rubber, the ball, the life span of which was very short, he stressed, not even the duration of a full match! Then he evoked the great Bill Tilden, who could serve like a demigod, he enthused, and dominated the tennis of the 1920s as no one ever would in his wake. In five years, Tilden did not lose a single match, and he walked off with the Davis Cup seven times in a row. He had what they used to call a cannonball serve, with a physique ideally suited for that sublime performance: tall, slender, with wide shoulders and huge hands. Ribbentrop embellished his shaggy-dog story with endless tidbits and anecdotes. For instance, Tilden, at the start of his most prolific series of victories, had had the tip of his finger amputated, after accidentally slicing it open on a fence. After the operation, he played better than ever, as if this little fingertip had been an error of natural selection that modern surgery had corrected. But more than anything, Tilden was a strategist—Ribbentrop stressed, wiping his lips on his napkin—and his book *The Art of Lawn Tennis* is a gold mine of reflections on tennis discipline, like Ovid's on the art of love. But especially—the quintessence of being, for the man his youthful friends had teasingly called "Ribbensnob"— Bill Tilden was nonchalant, so wonderfully nonchalant. And elegant: his backhand was like a reverence. On the courts, he reigned supreme. No one could touch him. Even his opponents' wins, when he was in his forties, did not oust him from first place, the place his regal style assured him in every match he played. Then Ribbentrop spoke about himself, his own game. Sir Alexander, truth be told, was finding all this tennis talk seriously boring, and he listened to the minister of the Reich with a fixed smile. Mrs. Chamberlain, too, had been trapped at the beginning of the meal and politely endured this flood of verbiage. Ribbentrop was now talking about his youthful visits to Canada, when in white shirt and trousers, wearing out his moccasins on the courts, he served aces practically at will. He even went so far as to stand up and mime a lob, almost knocking over a glass—but no, he caught it in time and it was laughed off as a joke. For a moment, he went back to Tilden, the twelve thousand people who had come to see him play around 1920, which was an absolute record for the time, and still today remains an astounding number. But more than anything, he remained *number one*, Ribbentrop reiterated several times, he remained *number one* for many years. Thank the Lord, the main course arrived just then.

As an appetizer, they had been served iced Charentais melon, and Ribbentrop had gobbled his down without paying it the slightest attention. The main dish was pullet from Louhans prepared à la Lucien Tendret. Winston Churchill complimented it and, perhaps as a joke on Ribbentrop and to tease Cadogan, he steered the Reich minister back to tennis. Hadn't this Bill Tilden also been an actor on Broadway, as well as the author of two wretched novels, *The Phantom Drive* and *The Pinch Quitter*—or something like that? Ribbentrop didn't know. In fact, there was much he didn't know about Bill Tilden.

The meal continued in the same vein. The Reich's ambassador seemed completely in his element. Moreover, it was his relaxed demeanor that had drawn Hitler's notice, his old-fashioned manners and elegance, in the midst of a Nazi Party mostly made up of ruffians and thugs. His regal attitude, coupled with an underlayer of perfect servility, had propelled him to the enviable post of Foreign Minister; and at that moment—on March 12, 1938, in Downing Street— he found himself at the zenith of what life would offer him. He had begun his professional career as an importer of Mumm and Pommery champagnes, and Hitler had sent him to England to lobby on behalf of the Reich, to sound people out and gather, where he could, useful bits of information. During that troubled period, he never stopped assuring Hitler that the English were incapable of responding. He consistently encouraged the Führer to pursue the most audacious courses of action, flattering his brutal, megalomaniacal tendencies. And so he had climbed the ladder of Nazi glory, the man Hitler called behind his back "the little champagne salesman"—for prejudices are hard to shake, even for the most assiduous wreckers of the social order.

*R*ight in the middle of lunch, as Churchill relates in his memoirs, a messenger from the Foreign Office was shown in. Perhaps they were divvying up one last chicken thigh, unless they had already moved on to the *corniotte* pastries served with lemonade, or were sampling a *tarte aux shions*: ¾ cup flour, 8 tbsp. butter, one or two eggs, a pinch of salt, a little sugar, half a pint of milk, semolina, and some water to help blend it all. I'll skip over the details of how to cook and garnish this Louhans specialty. For they made a number of French dishes at Downing Street; the Prime Minister, Neville Chamberlain, was particularly fond of them. And why shouldn't he take an interest in cooking? It's written, somewhere in the *Historia Augusta*, that the Roman Senate used to deliberate for hours about which sauce to serve with turbot. It was thus between two clinks of a fork that the Foreign Office messenger quietly handed Alexander Cadogan an envelope. There was an awkward silence. Sir Alexander seemed to be reading carefully. The conversation slowly resumed. Ribbentrop, acting as if nothing had happened, murmured a few compliments to the lady of the house. At that point, Cadogan stood up and brought the note to Chamberlain. He seemed neither surprised nor put out by what he had just read. He was pensive. Chamberlain read it in turn, looking preoccupied. During this time, Ribbentrop kept on chattering. Dessert had just been served, marinated wild strawberries Escoffier-style, a true delicacy. They were consumed eagerly and Cadogan returned to his seat, taking back the note. But Churchill, training one of his big cocker spaniel eyes on Chamberlain, noticed a deep crease between the prime minister's brows; he surmised a worrisome development. Ribbentrop, for his part, noticed nothing. He was enjoying himself, no doubt carried away by the thrill of becoming a minister himself. At Mrs. Chamberlain's invitation, they moved on to the drawing room.

Coffee was served. Ribbentrop then began discoursing on French wines, his specialty, and for a long while he propped up the flagging conversation. To illustrate who knows what point, he snatched up an invisible flute set atop its invisible pyramid of glasses, and with great flourish proposed a toast. The invisible flute was cool to the touch, the invisible champagne chilled to an ideal forty-three degrees Fahrenheit. His dessert knife tapped on the flute; Ribbentrop nodded and smiled. Outside it had rained and the trees were wet, the sidewalks glistening.

The Chamberlains showed some impatience, but politely. You cannot just cut short a reception of this kind, with the minister of a European power. You need tact, a way to exit gracefully. Before long, the guests, too, no doubt started to realize that something was amiss, and that a subterranean conversation was being held between Chamberlain and his wife, which drew in the other protagonists one by one: Cadogan, the Churchills, a few others. The first guests made their excuses. But the Ribbentrops remained in place, oblivious to the general malaise—he especially, whom that farewell event seemed to have intoxicated and deprived of the most rudimentary manners. They grew impatient—though again, very politely, without letting it show. They couldn't very well throw the guest of honor out the door, now could they? He just had to realize on his own that the time had come to leave, put on his overcoat, and climb back into his big swastikaed Mercedes.

But Ribbentrop did not realize a thing, not a blessed thing; he kept on jabbering. And his wife, too, had just engaged Mrs. Chamberlain in lively conversation. The atmosphere became unreal; the guests indicated, by very subtle inflections of voice, restlessness that was barely perceptible, but that should have been discernible to a well-bred person. At such moments,

ÉRIC VUILLARD

we can't help wondering if we are crazy or just overly considerate, and whether the other person feels the embarrassment we experience so keenly. But no, nothing. The brain is an airtight organ. Our eyes do not give away our thoughts, and imperceptible changes of expression are illegible to others. It's as if our entire body were a poem that consumed us, but of which our neighbors didn't understand a word.

Suddenly, taking the situation in hand, Chamberlain said to Ribbentrop, "I am sorry, I have to go now to attend to urgent business." It was a bit abrupt, but it was the best way he could find of ending it. Everyone stood up, and most of the guests thanked their hosts and left Downing Street. But the Ribbentrops lingered with the few who remained. The discussion dragged on awhile longer. No one mentioned the note that Cadogan and Chamberlain had read during lunch, which floated between them like a little paper ghost, an unknown retort that everyone wanted to hear, and which was in fact the true script of that bizarre vaudeville. Finally, everyone took their leave, but not before Ribbentrop had run through his entire repertoire of insipid small talk. It's just that the onetime amateur actor was playing one of his secret roles on the great stage of History. A former ice skater, golfer, violinist—that Ribbentrop could do anything! Everything! Even stretch out an official luncheon to absurd lengths. He was an odd duck, that one, a curious mix of ignorance and refinement. Apparently, he made awful grammatical errors—errors that his rival von Neurath, when he read the memoranda that Ribbentrop composed for the Führer's attention, scrupulously neglected to correct.

The very last guests took their leave, and the Ribbentrop couple finally cleared off. Their driver opened the door for them. Frau Ribbentrop delicately folded back her dress and they got into the car. And then they let their hair down. The Ribbentrops had a good laugh at the trick they'd played on everyone. They had, of course, noticed that once Chamberlain read the note sent by the Foreign Office, he seemed preoccupied, terribly preoccupied. And of course, the Ribbentrops knew exactly what was in that note, and had deliberately set out to make Chamberlain, and the rest of his gang, waste as much time as possible. They had prolonged the meal ad infinitum, then the coffee, then the drawing room conversations, testing the limits of reason. During that time, Chamberlain, instead of attending to urgent business, had been kept busy with tennis talk and macarons. Playing off his excessive politeness, so excessive that it was almost a sickness, a politeness that kept even affairs of state waiting, the Ribbentrops had very cleverly distracted him from his work. Because that note brought by the Foreign Office envoy, the mystery of which hovered over the entire luncheon, contained the dreadful news that German troops had just crossed into Austria.

BLITZKRIEG

*O*n the morning of March 12, Austria waited feverishly and with indecent joy for the Germans to arrive. In many films of the time, we see people stretching their hands toward the window of a kiosk or panel truck to get a swastika flag. Everywhere, people stood on tiptoe, hoisted themselves onto ledges and walls, climbed up lampposts, anywhere they could, just so they could *see*. But the Germans let them wait. Morning passed, then afternoon…very strange. Now and then the sound of an engine roared over the countryside, flags waved, smiles blossomed on faces. "They're coming! They're coming!" could be heard from every direction. Wide eyes were glued to the road—and then nothing. They kept up hope for a while longer, then relaxed, arms limp, and fifteen minutes later they were on the ground again, squatting in the grass, chatting.

For the evening of the twelfth, the Viennese Nazis had planned a torchlight tattoo to welcome Adolf Hitler. The ceremony would be stirring and grand. They waited until late in the day, but no one came. They didn't understand what was going on. Men guzzled beer and bellowed out songs, but after a while they didn't really feel like singing anymore and instead just felt vaguely disappointed. So when three German soldiers got off the train, there was a moment of jubilation. German soldiers? A miracle! They were the guests of the entire city; no one had ever loved them as much as the Viennese did that night! Vienna! They were offered every chocolate, every pine branch, all the water in the Danube, all the wind from the Carpathians, your Ringstrasse, your Schönbrunn Palace, its Chinese Cabinets, its Napoleon Room, the body of the King of Rome, the saber from the Battle of the Pyramids! All of it! And yet, they were just three little soldiers sent to arrange billeting for the troops. But everyone was so impatient to be invaded that they were paraded around the city and carried in triumph. And the three poor dopes couldn't really understand the enthusiasm they had sparked.

They had no idea anyone could love them so fiercely. They were even a bit nervous: love can be scary. And then the questions started. People began wondering, Where was the German war machine? What happened to the tanks? The armored cars? All those fabulous beasts we'd been promised—where were they? Didn't the Führer want his native Austria anymore? No, no, it wasn't that, but... A rumor started spreading, one they didn't dare say aloud—you had to be careful with those Nazis, who listened in on everything. They said— nothing certain, mind you, but the situation seemed to bear out the gossip—that after having crossed the border like lightning, the fabulous German war machine had come to a crashing halt.

In fact, the German army had had quite a time getting over the border. It had taken place in inde- scribable chaos and with astounding slowness. At the moment, they were stuck near Linz, an advance of barely sixty miles. And yet, the weather was apparently quite pleasant that March 12, even ideal.

It had all started off so well! At nine that morn- ing, they simply lifted the border guard's barrier and there they were, in Austria! No need for violence or bombshells. It was all very loving; they conquered gently, effortlessly, and with a smile. The tanks, trucks, heavy artillery, the whole kit and caboodle lumbered slowly toward Vienna for the great courtship dance. The bride was willing; this was no rape, as some have claimed, but a proper wedding. The Austrians shouted themselves hoarse, made their best Nazi salutes as a sign of welcome; they had been practicing for five years. But the road to Linz was arduous, vehicles tipped over, motorcycles sputtered like lawn mowers. Those Germans would have been better off gardening, making a little tour of Austria and then heading quietly back to Berlin; turning all this junk into tractors and planting cabbages in the Tiergarten. For as they approached Linz, everything went south. And still the sky was cloudless, calm, the most beautiful sky imaginable.

The horoscope on March 12 was highly favorable for Libra, Cancer, and Scorpio, but disastrous for everyone else. Against the invasion, the European democracies offered only mesmerized resignation. The British government, aware of its imminence, had notified Schuschnigg. That was all it did. The French, for their part, had no government, having just been hit with a ministerial crisis.

In Vienna, that morning of March 12, only the editor in chief of the *Neues Wiener Tagblatt*, Emil Löbl, would publish an article in praise of the little dictator Schuschnigg—a rather puny act of defiance, and practically the only one. Later that morning, a mob appeared at the newspaper and forced Löbl off the premises. The SA burst into the offices and beat up staff, reporters, and editors. Yet they were hardly lefties at the *Neues Wiener*. They hadn't made a sound when the Parliament went up in smoke, had quietly approved the authoritarian Catholicism of the new regime, accepted the editorial purges under Dollfuss, and the suppression of the Social Democrats, who were jailed or barred from working, did not trouble them much. But heroism is a strange, relative thing, and that morning, all in all, it is both moving and disturbing to see that Emil Löbl was the only man to protest.

In Linz, it was no different. They had carried out horrible purges, and by now the city was all-Nazi. Everywhere they were singing breathlessly, hoping at any moment to witness the arrival of the Führer. Everyone seemed to be there; the sun shone and the beer flowed. Then the morning was over, people dozed off in the corner of a bar, and since nothing can stop time, it was suddenly noon and the sun hit its zenith over the Pöstlingberg. The fountains fell silent, families went home for lunch, the Danube rolled its waves. In the botanical gardens, the fabulous cacti were littered with confetti, which the spiders mistook for flies. In Vienna, at the bar of the Grand Café, there was talk that the Germans hadn't yet reached Wels, maybe not even Meggenhofen! Some wiseacres cracked that they'd gotten their directions mixed up and were heading off toward Suse or Damietta, that they'd find them next year at the Bobino concert hall! But some whispered that they'd had a breakdown, were short of fuel, faced huge problems getting fresh supplies.

———

*H*itler left Munich by car, the icy wind whipping his face. His Mercedes drove through the deep forests. He had planned to stop first in Braunau, his hometown, then in Linz, the city of his youth, and finally in Leonding, where his parents were buried—a nostalgia trip, basically. At around four in the afternoon, Hitler had crossed the border at Braunau. The weather was sunny but very cold; his procession was made up of twenty-four cars and around twenty trucks. Everyone was there: the SS, the SA, the police, every branch of the army. They communed with the crowd. They stopped for a moment in front of the Führer's birthplace, but there was no time to lose! They were already late. Little girls held out bouquets, the crowd waved swastika flags, everything was going great. By midafternoon, the procession had already passed through a host of villages. Hitler smiled, waved, his elation visible on his face. He gave the National Socialist salute at every opportunity, to vague clusters of peasants or teenage girls. But most often, he contented himself with the gesture Chaplin parodied so well, arm folded in a lackadaisical, almost feminine pose.

PANZER BLOCKAGE

Blitzkrieg is a simple slogan, a label that publicists slapped onto disaster. The theoretician behind this aggressive strategy was named Heinz Guderian. In one of his books, the sharply and strikingly titled *Achtung—Panzer!*, Guderian developed his doctrine of lightning war. Naturally, he had read J. F. C. Fuller, adored his inane book on yoga, feverishly devoured his stark raving prophecies, in which he thought he discovered the horrific mysteries of the world. But it was especially the writings on mechanized warfare that kept Guderian up at night. Fuller's little tomes gave him much food for thought; their passionate evocation of war as brutal and heroic spoke to him. For John Frederick Charles Fuller was a passionate man, so passionate that not long afterward he would join Oswald Mosley in deploring the indolence of the parliamentary democracies and calling for a more rousing form of government. He became a member of the Nordic League, which aimed at promoting Nazism. The little council met in secret, in some very British cottage or other, and spent long hours talking about the Jews. But its sympathizers weren't just some Mayfair merchants: they also counted among their number Lady Douglas-Hamilton, the famous animal lover—for as the saying goes, the human soul is the seat of all miseries. There was also the good Duke of Wellington, Arthur Wellesley, the darling of the salons and an Old Etonian, who had enjoyed every privilege and therefore had no excuse. A connoisseur of Propertius and Lucan, who no doubt took his strolls at dawn over the grounds of his estate, huffing on his panpipe among the shepherds of Theocritus. A collector of art—admittedly not very good art, but even so. A man with a narrow skull, weak mouth, and an empty gaze; the kind of person who, had he been born in a modest London suburb, would not have been given a second look.

———

Achtung—Panzer! On March 12, 1938, the armored tanks led the parade. At the head of the XVI Army Corps, Heinz Guderian was finally about to see his dream come true. The first German tank had been built in 1918, in a run of twenty; it was a heavy metal carcass, a two-hundred-horsepower box, a fat baby-buggy, slow and cumbersome to maneuver. At the end of the First World War, one of them met an English tank in head-to-head combat and was blown to smithereens. While tanks had made significant progress since that first baptism of fire, there was still a long way to go. The Panzer IV, which for a time would be the queen of the battlefield, was in its infancy on that day in March 1938. Produced by Krupp, that little tank was a rather mediocre war machine. Its armor was too light, unable to withstand antitank shells, and its gun was effective only on soft targets. The Panzer II was even smaller, a real sardine can. It was quick and nimble, but it couldn't pierce the armor of an enemy tank, while remaining vulnerable itself. It was obsolete the minute it rolled out of the factory. In fact, it had been intended only for training purposes, but production lagged, war was declared sooner than expected, and it was put into active service. As for the Panzer I, it was really just a tankette, with room for only two men who sat directly on the metal floor, like yoga instructors. It was too fragile and its armament too weak, but at least it was cheap to make—hardly more expensive than a tractor.

The Versailles Treaty had forbidden Germany from manufacturing tanks, so German factories produced them through shell companies abroad. Creative accounting has always underwritten the most toxic maneuvers. In secret, then, Germany had built itself a prodigious war machine, or so they said. And it was precisely that new army, that promise finally fulfilled in broad daylight, that all of Austria was awaiting by the roadside on March 12, 1938. And so they must have been getting a bit worried, a bit anxious under the dazzling sky.

*I*t was then that the formidable German war machine hit a snag. First there was an entire line of tanks motionless on the side of the road. Hitler, whose Mercedes had to go around them, glared contemptuously. Then came other heavy artillery vehicles, stalled in the middle of the road; and they could honk their horns all they liked and yell that the Führer had to pass—the tanks remained stuck. A motor is a sublime thing, a real miracle if you think about it. A bit of fuel, a spark—pressure builds up, pushes the piston, which makes the crankshaft turn, and bam, off you go. But in fact, it's only simple on paper, and when it stops working, what a shit-storm! None of it makes any sense. You have to stick your hands in a dirty, oily mess, unscrew this, tighten that...And that March 12, despite the blazing sun, it was cold as all get-out. So it was no fun dragging your toolbox along the side of the road. Hitler was fit to be tied: what was supposed to be his day of glory, a swift, spellbinding passage, had morphed into a traffic jam. Instead of speed there was congestion; instead of vitality, asphyxiation; instead of a surge, a bottleneck.

In the small towns of Altheim and Reid, and pretty much everywhere else, young Austrians waited, their faces reddened by the wind. Some of them wept from the cold. Back then, in the great round-robin of celebrities, the French cheered for Tino Rossi at the Galeries Lafayette and the Americans swung to the tunes of Benny Goodman. But the Austrian girls didn't give a hoot for Tino Rossi or Benny Goodman: they wanted Adolf Hitler. And so, you could regularly hear them screaming on the way into town, *"Der Führer kommt!"* And then, when nothing came, they went back to chatting about this and that.

For it wasn't only a few isolated tanks that had broken down, not just the occasional armored car— no, it was the vast majority of the great German army, and the road was now entirely blocked. It was like a slapstick comedy! A purple-faced Führer, mechanics running around the roadside, orders being yelled back and forth in the harsh, feverish idiom of the Third Reich. And besides, when an army hurls itself at you, parades by at twenty miles per hour under the brilliant sun, it can be quite a show. But when an army's out of order, it doesn't look like much. A broken-down army is guaranteed ridicule. And man, did the general get raked over the coals! Screams, insults. Hitler holds him responsible for this fiasco. They had to shove aside some of the heavy vehicles, tow away a few tanks, and push some cars so the Führer could get through. He finally arrived in Linz after nightfall.

*D*uring this time, beneath the icy moon, the German troops loaded as many tanks as they could onto railway cars. They no doubt rushed in engineers and crane operators from Munich. And so the trains hauled away the armor the way you'd transport circus equipment. They simply had to be in Vienna in time for the official ceremonies, the grand spectacle! It must have been a bizarre scene, those sinister silhouettes, those trains rolling across nighttime Austria like hearses, with their cargo of armored cars and tanks.

WIRETAPS

On March 13, the day after the Anschluss, the British Secret Service intercepted a curious telephone farce between England and Germany: "Mister Ribbentrop," complained Goering, who was looking after the Reich while Hitler flew back to his homeland, "the story about our having given an ultimatum to Austria is, of course, nonsense. Schuschnigg is lying. It was Seyss-Inquart, brought to power by popular demand, who asked us to send troops. If you knew how brutal the Schuschnigg regime has been!" And Ribbentrop came back with, "That's incredible! Why, the whole world must know of this!" The conversation continued in this vein for a good half hour. And we can only imagine the faces of those who were jotting down those peculiar statements, and who must have felt like they were standing backstage at a theater. Then the dialogue ended. Goering spoke of the lovely weather. The blue sky. The twittering birds. He was standing on his balcony, he said, listening on the radio to the enthusiasm of the Austrians. "Oh, that is marvelous!" exclaimed Ribbentrop.

Seven years later, on November 29, 1945, the same dialogue was heard. The same words, perhaps a bit less hesitant, more written out, but exactly the same casual phrases and sense of mockery. This took place at the International Military Tribunal in Nuremberg. The American prosecutor, Sidney S. Alderman, to buttress his indictment of crimes against peace, pulled a sheaf of papers from his folder. The conversation between Ribbentrop and Goering seemed very illuminating to him. They used a kind of "double talk," he said, intended to mislead other nations.

Alderman then began to read. He read the little dialogue as one might read the lines of a play, so much so that when he spoke Goering's name, as a character in the script, the real Goering seated in the prisoners' dock began to rise. But he soon realized he was not being called. They were simply going to play his part right there in front of him and read out his tirades. In a heavy, monotonous voice, Alderman recited:

> GOERING: You know already that the Führer has charged me with the running of the Government, and I thought I would ring you and give you all the necessary information. The jubilation in Austria is indescribable— you can hear that on the radio.
>
> RIBBENTROP: Yes, it is fantastic, isn't it?
>
> GOERING: Seyss-Inquart—who at this time was already in charge of the Government—asked us to invade immediately. We were already at the border with our troops because we could not know in advance whether there would be civil war or not, you see?

But what Goering didn't know at the time, on March 13, 1938, was that one day someone would get hold of more truthful exchanges. He had asked his own secretaries to take down his significant conversations; it was important that someday History should inherit them. Who knows, perhaps in his old age he'd write his own *Gallic Wars*. And he would base it on notes taken on the fly at major moments in his career. What he didn't predict was that those notes, instead of sitting in his desk drawer after his retirement, would end up in the hands of a prosecutor at Nuremberg. And so we can hear other scenes, those played out between Berlin and Vienna two days earlier, on the night of March 11, when he thought no one was listening but Seyss-Inquart, or Dombrowski of the German embassy in Vienna, who acted as go-between, and of course, the person who was taking down their momentous conversations for posterity. He didn't know that in reality, the whole world was listening in. Maybe not while he was actually speaking, but from the future, from that very posterity he had in mind. That's the way it is. All the conversations Goering held that evening are scrupulously archived and available. Miraculously, the bombs spared them.

GOERING: When will Seyss-Inquart have formed the new cabinet?

DOMBROWSKI: Oh, perhaps by nine-fifteen p.m.

GOERING: The cabinet must be formed by seven-thirty.

DOMBROWSKI: Seven-thirty. Yes, sir.

GOERING: Keppler will bring you the names.
The Austrian Army is to be taken by Seyss-Inquart himself and you know who gets the Justice Department.

DOMBROWSKI: Oh, yes, indeed.

GOERING: Tell me his name.

DOMBROWSKI: Well, your brother-in-law, isn't it?

GOERING: That's right.

Hour after hour, Goering dictates his orders. Step by step. And in the brevity of the replies, we can hear his imperious tone, his disdain. The Mafioso aspect of the whole business is plain to see. Barely twenty minutes after the above scene, Seyss-Inquart calls. Goering orders him to go back and make Miklas understand that if he does not name Seyss-Inquart chancellor before seven-thirty, German troops will march and Austria will cease to exist. This is a far cry from the nice little exchange between Goering and Ribbentrop for the English spies' benefit, a far cry from the liberators of Austria. And still another thing draws our attention: Goering's choice of expression, the threat of Austria *ceasing to exist*. They go straight for the most extreme formulations. To fully appreciate this, we have to rewind the tape, forget what we think we know, forget about the war, set aside the newsreels of the time, Goebbels's montages and all his propaganda. We have to remind ourselves that, at that moment, *Blitzkrieg* was nothing. It was just a bunch of stalled Panzers. Just a monstrous traffic jam on the Austrian highways, some furious men, a word that was coined later, like a gamble. What's astounding about this war is the remarkable triumph of bravado, from which we can infer one lesson: everyone is susceptible to a *bluff*. Even the strictest, most serious, most old-world souls: they might not give in to the demands of justice, they might not yield to an insurgent populace, but they'll always fold before a bluff.

———

*I*n Nuremberg, Goering listened to Alderman's recital with his chin resting on his fist. Now and then, he smiled. The protagonists of the play were all gathered in the same room. They were no longer in Berlin, Vienna, and London, but mere yards from one another: Ribbentrop and his farewell luncheon, Seyss-Inquart and his kapo toadyism, Goering and his gangster methods. Finally, to conclude his demonstration, Alderman returned to the thirteenth of March. He read the end of the brief dialogue. He read it in a monotonous tone that stripped it of all prestige and reduced it to what it was: pure and simple sleaze.

> GOERING: The weather here in Berlin is
> wonderful. Blue skies! I am sitting here
> wrapped up in blankets on my terrace in
> the bracing air and drinking my coffee. The
> birds are twittering, and every now and then
> I can hear through the radio the outburst of
> joy and jubilation over there. It is colossal.
> RIBBENTROP: Oh, that is marvelous!

At that moment, beneath the huge clock face, in the prisoners' dock, time stopped; something happened. The whole room turned to look. As reported by Kessel, *France-Soir*'s special correspondent to the Nuremberg trials, when Goering heard the word *marvelous*, he burst out laughing. At the memory of that overplayed exclamation, perhaps sensing how dissonant that stagey bit of dialogue was with History-capital-H, with its decency, the image it conveys of great events, Goering looked at Ribbentrop and guffawed. And Ribbentrop, too, was shaken by nervous laughter. Sitting opposite the international tribunal, opposite their judges, opposite journalists from the world over, amid the ruins, they could not help laughing.

THE PROP SHOP

*T*ruth is scattered into many kinds of dust. Well before he took the pseudonym Anders ("Otherwise"), the German intellectual Günther Stern, who had immigrated to the United States, poor, Jewish, living off odd jobs, became a prop man when he was in his forties. He worked at the Hollywood Custom Palace, whose showrooms harbored the entire sartorial history of humankind. The Hollywood Custom Palace rented costumes to movie studios. Outfits for Cleopatra or Danton, medieval jugglers or Burghers of Calais. You could find anything there, all of humanity's castoffs, scraps of glory lying on the shelves, sham memories. Wooden swords, cardboard crowns, paper walls—everything was fake: the coal dust on a miner's collar, the wear on the knees of a beggar's pants, the blood on a convict's neck. History as spectacle. At the Hollywood Palace, you would come across everything that had been, without distinction: martyrs' rags hung out to dry with patricians' togas. They say that images, movies, photos are not the real world, but I'm not so sure. The twelve stories of this colossus, featuring heaps of garments from different eras, leave an impression of absurdity or folly. As if we were at the heart of grandeur, but wedged in, shrunken; as if dust were only powder, wear only illusion, filth merely makeup, and appearance the reality of things. But all of humanity—that's excessive. The Hollywood Palace piled up too many castoffs, amassed too many variants, accumulated too many epochs. You could find B-movie Roman, tacky Egyptian, circus Babylonian, contraband Greek, as well as every variety of loincloth and legging, colored saris for women of Gujarat, rich Baluchari silk from Bengal, light cotton from Pondicherry, and Malayan sarongs. You could dig out ponchos, hooded cloaks, paenulae, early sleeved garments, tunics, shirts, blouses, caftans, the skins of prehistoric beasts, and all manner of trousers. It was a magic cave, that Hollywood Palace. Of course, working there was not exactly glamorous: folding the clothes of Pancho Villa's corpse, altering Mary Stuart's collar, putting Napoleon's hat back on the shelf. But still, what a privilege to be History's prop man.

In his diary, Günther Stern stressed that they had it all, from the outfits of circus animals to Adam's fig leaf to SA jackboots. But what's most surprising is not that you could find so many costumes, but that you could *already* find the costumes of Nazis. And the irony, as Stern noted, was that a Jew was shining their boots. Because all those togs had to be maintained. And like any other employee of the Hollywood Palace, Günther Stern had to polish the Nazis' boots as scrupulously as he brushed gladiators' buskins or Chinese sandals. No place for real drama here, the costumes had to be ready for the shoot, for the great stage production of the world. And ready they would be. And they were truer than life, more exact than the ones hanging in museums. Perfect replicas, missing not a button or a thread, and available in every size, just like in clothing stores. But also threadbare, dirty, ripped and torn. Because after all, the world was not a fashion show, and the movies had to create an illusion. So they also had to maintain false rips, false rust. They had to give the impression of time having passed.

And so, well before the Battle of Stalingrad was fought, before Operation Barbarossa was being planned, before the French campaign was a twinkle in the Germans' eye, the war was already there, on the shelves of showbiz. The great American machine was already capitalizing on the upheaval. The war would become only an exploit to be recounted and turned into revenue. A theme. A profitable deal. In the final account, it was not the Panzers, or the Stukas, or Stalin's organs that changed the face of the world, remodeled and creased it. It was over a few square blocks of industrious California, at the intersection of a donut shop and a gas station, that the substance of our lives gained its tone of collective certainty. It was there, in the first supermarkets, in front of the first TV sets, between the toaster and the pocket calculator, that the world's story was told with its true cadence, the one it would adopt forever after.

And while the Führer was busy preparing his attack on France, while his general staff was still dithering with Schlieffen's outmoded plans and his mechanics were still repairing their Panzers, Hollywood had already deposited their costumes on the shelves of the past. They were on the hangers of yesterday's news, folded and piled on the rack with the other old junk. Well before the war had begun, while blind, deaf Lebrun was signing his decrees about the lottery, while Halifax was aiding and abetting, and the frightened population of Austria entrusted its hopes for the future to a raving lunatic, the costumes of Nazi soldiers were already on markdown at the prop shop.

THE SOUND OF MUSIC

*O*n March 15, in front of the imperial palace, covering the entire surface of the plaza and even on the great equestrian statue of Archduke Charles, the crowds, the poor crowds of Austria, abused, mistreated, but ultimately acquiescent, came to cheer. If we lift the hideous rags of History, we find this: hierarchy versus equality, and order versus liberty. And so, misled by a petty and dangerous idea of nationhood, one with no future, this vast crowd, frustrated by a prior defeat, thrust their arms in the air. There, on the balcony of Sissi's palace, speaking in a voice that was terribly strange, lyrical, and disturbing, ending with a hoarse, unpleasant cry, was Hitler. He screamed in a German very close to the language later invented by Chaplin, full of vituperations, in which they could make out only a few scattered words: *war, Jews, world.* The multitudes roared. The Führer had just declared the Anschluss from the balcony. The cheering was so unanimous, so powerful, so fulsome, that we might well wonder if it isn't always the same crowd we hear in the newsreels of the time, the same soundtrack. For those are the films we watch; those newsreels and propaganda sequences are what show us this history, shape our intimate knowledge of it. All our thinking derives from this homogeneous backdrop.

We can never know. We no longer know who's speaking. The films of that time have become our memories, as if through some horrendous magic spell. The world war and its preamble are swept along in this endless movie, leaving us unable to distinguish between true and false. And since the Reich recruited more film-makers, directors, cameramen, sound engineers, and stagehands than any other protagonist in this drama, we can say that our images of the war, at least before the Russians and Americans entered it, will forever be directed by Joseph Goebbels. History unspools before our eyes, like a film by Joseph Goebbels. It's extraordinary. German newsreels become an exemplary fiction. As such, the Anschluss looks like a phenomenal

ÉRIC VUILLARD

success. But the cheering was evidently added to the images, dubbed. And it's quite possible that none of the insane ovations that greeted the Führer's appearances are among the ones we've actually heard.

I've watched those films again. No question that Nazi militants were brought in from all over the country, while dissidents and Jews were arrested—it's a handpicked crowd. But still, those are Austrians there, not a throng of extras. Those joyful young girls with their blond braids are indeed there, as is the couple who shouts while beaming—oh, all those smiles, all those waves! The banners quivering as the motorcade passes! Not a single shot was fired. How sad!

$\mathcal{T}$hings had not gone entirely as planned, of course: the "best army in the world" had just demonstrated that it was still no more than an assemblage of metal, hollow sheet metal. And yet, despite the lack of preparation; despite the defective equipment; despite the fact that, not long before, the zeppelin *Hindenburg* had burst into flames while docking in New Jersey, killing thirty-five passengers; despite the fact that most generals of the Luftwaffe still knew little about combat aviation, and that Hitler appointed himself supreme military commander without any experience—despite all this, the newsreels of the time give the impression of a relentless machine. In these newsreels, in cleverly framed sequences, we see German tanks advancing amid jubilant crowds. Who could imagine that they'd broken down only a short while before? The German army seemed to march on the path to victory, a simple victory, paved with flowers and smiles. Suetonius tells us that the Roman emperor Caligula had similarly transported his legions to the North, and that during a momentary lapse or giddy spell, he lined them up facing the sea and ordered them to gather shells. Watching the French newsreels, one gets the impression that the German soldiers had spent their day collecting smiles.

*S*ometimes it seems that what happens to us was written in a newspaper that is already several months old, or is a bad dream we've already had. Barely six months later, six months after the Anschluss, on September 29, 1938, we find ourselves back in Munich for the famous conference. And as if Hitler's appetites could be sated, they gave away Czechoslovakia. The French and English delegations went to Germany. They were well received. In the great hall, the chandelier tinkled; the crystal pendants, like wind chimes ruffled by the breeze, played their aerial score above the heads of the bogeymen. Daladier's and Chamberlain's teams tried to wrest from Hitler a few picayune concessions.

We shower History with abuse, claiming that it makes the protagonists of our torments strike poses. We never see the grimy hem, the yellowed tablecloth, the check stub, the coffee ring. We only get to see events from their good side. Still, if we look closely, on the photo showing Chamberlain and Daladier in Munich beside Hitler and Mussolini, just before signing the agreement, the English and French prime ministers do not look very pleased with themselves. Nevertheless, they signed. After rolling down the streets of Munich under the cheers of the masses, who welcomed them with Nazi salutes, they signed. And we can see them in the newsreels: Daladier, chapeau on his head, looking a little sheepish, saying hello to the camera; Chamberlain, hat in hand, with a broad grin. That tireless "artisan of peace," as the newspapers of the time dubbed him, stands on the steps, for all black-and-white eternity, between two rows of Nazi soldiers.

Meanwhile, the enthusiastic announcer intones nasally that the four heads of state, Daladier, Chamberlain, Mussolini, and Hitler, driven by the same devotion to peace, are posing for posterity. History reveals the deplorable meaninglessness of this commentary and discredits all future news reports. They say that Munich inspired great hope, but those who say it don't know what words mean. They speak a utopian language in which, supposedly, all words are equal. Not long afterward, Édouard Daladier, on Radio Paris, 1648 meters (182 kHz) over longwave, after a few notes of music, spoke. He was convinced of having saved peace in Europe: that's what he said. But he didn't believe it for a second. "Those morons,

ÉRIC VUILLARD

if only they knew!" he apparently muttered as he got off the plane to the cheering crowds. This great jumble of misery, in which horrific events are already taking shape, is dominated by a mysterious respect for lies. Political maneuvering tramples facts. And the declarations of our leaders will soon be blown away like tin roofs in a hurricane.

THE DEAD

*I*n order to sanction the annexation of Austria, they held a referendum. They arrested the few remaining dissidents. From their pulpits, priests called upon the faithful to vote Nazi, and the churches bedecked themselves in swastika banners. Even the former leader of the Social Democrats endorsed a "yes" vote. There were practically no dissenting voices. Ninety-nine point seven-five percent of Austrians voted in favor of incorporation into the Reich. And while the twenty-four gents from the beginning of our tale, the high priests of German industry, were already studying how to carve up the country, Hitler had made what we could call a triumphant tour of Austria. On the occasion of that fantastic homecoming, he had been cheered everywhere he went.

And yet, just before the Anschluss, there were more than one thousand seven hundred suicides in a single week. Soon, reporting a suicide in the press would become an act of resistance. A few journalists still dared to write "sudden demise," but swift reprisals quickly silenced them. They looked for alternative, safe expressions. And so, the actual number of those who took their lives remains unknown, as do their names. The day after the annexation, we could still read these four obituaries in the *Neue Freie Presse*: "On March 12, in the morning, Alma Biro, civil servant, age 40, slit her wrists with a razor and turned on the gas. At the same moment, the writer Karl Schlesinger, age 49, shot himself in the head. A housewife, Helene Kuhner, age 69, also committed suicide. That afternoon, Leopold Bien, civil servant, 36, leapt from a window. We are unaware of his motives for this act." This bland annotation is shameful. For on March 13, no one could have been unaware of their motives. No one. Moreover, it's not about individual motives, but about a single, shared cause.

Alma, Karl, Leopold, or Helene might have seen, from their windows, the Jews being dragged along the streets. They would only have needed to glimpse those whose heads had been shaved in order to understand. They would only have needed to see the man on whose head a Tau cross had been painted, the cross of the Crusaders, which Chancellor Schuschnigg had worn on his lapel just one hour earlier. Even before this, it would have been enough to hear it, to guess it, to intuit it, to imagine it. It would have been enough to see the smiles on people's faces in order to know.

And what difference does it make whether, that morning, Helene did or didn't see the Jews down on all fours amid the bellowing crowds, forced to scrub the sidewalks under the mocking eyes of passersby? What difference whether or not she witnessed the vile scenes of them being made to eat grass? Her death expresses only what she felt, the great sorrow, the hideous reality, her disgust with a world that she had seen display itself in all its murderous nudity. For ultimately, the crime was already there, in the little pennants, the smiles on girls' faces, in that entire perverted spring. And even in the laughter, in that unchained fervor, Helene Kuhner must have felt the hatred and the giddiness. Behind those thousands of silhouettes and faces, she must have glimpsed, in a terrifying rush, the millions of prisoners. She must have divined, behind the horrifying jubilation, the granite quarry of Mauthausen. And then she saw herself dying. In the smiles of the young women of Vienna, on March 12, 1938, in the midst of the shouting crowds, in the fresh scent of forget-me-nots, in the heart of that weird mirth and all that fervor, she must have experienced a black grief.

Streamers, confetti, pennants. Whatever became of those young girls and their wild enthusiasm? What became of their smiles, their carefree faces so earnest and joyful? And all that jubilation from March 1938? If today one of them were suddenly to recognize herself on-screen, what would she think? Our true thoughts have always been secret, since the beginning of time. We think in apocopes, apneas. Underneath, life flows like sap, slow and subterranean. But now that wrinkles have gnawed at her mouth, made her eyelids iridescent, dampened her voice—her eyes skimming over surfaces, between the television spitting out its archival images and the yogurt, while the clueless nurse goes about her business with nary a thought for the

World War, the generations having succeeded one another like sentinels in the dark night—how does she separate the youth she lived, the scent of fruit, that breathless rise of sap, from the horror? I don't know. And in her retirement home, amid the insipid odors of ether and iodine, in her birdlike fragility, does the wrinkled, aged child—recognizing herself in the film clip, in the cold light of the TV screen, she who has survived the war, the ruins, the American or Russian occupation, with her slippers trailing on the linoleum, her warm liver-spotted hands falling slowly from the rattan armrests when the nurse opens the door—does she sigh sometimes, extracting the painful memories from their formaldehyde?

Alma Biro, Karl Schlesinger, Leopold Bien, and Helene Kuhner did not live that long. Before throwing himself from the window, on March 12, 1938, Leopold must have confronted the truth several times, then the shame. Wasn't he, too, an Austrian? And hadn't he supported, for years, the grotesque farce of National Catholicism? When two Austrian Nazis rang at his door that afternoon, the young man's face suddenly looked very old. For some time, he had been seeking new words that would express something other than authority and violence; but he couldn't find any. He spent entire days wandering the streets, fearful of meeting a hostile neighbor, a former colleague who would look away. The life he loved had ceased to exist. Nothing was left: neither his pride in his work, which he took pleasure in doing well, nor his frugal lunch, which he ate while people-watching on the steps of an old building. Everything had been destroyed. And so, on that afternoon of March 12, when his buzzer rang, his thoughts enveloped him in fog, and for an instant he heard that faint inner voice that always resists long intoxications of the soul. He opened the window and jumped.

In a letter to Margarete Steffin, with a feverish sarcasm that time and postwar revelations make unbearable, Walter Benjamin relates how they had suddenly cut off the gas for Vienna's Jews: their consumption was costing the gas company too much money. The biggest consumers were precisely the ones who never paid their bills, he adds. At that point, Benjamin's letter to Margarete takes a strange turn. We're not sure we've understood correctly. We hesitate. Its meaning floats amid the branches, in the pale sky, and when it becomes clear, suddenly forming a little pool of sense out of nowhere, it becomes one of the saddest and most insane statements of all time. For if the Austrian gas company refused to provide service to the Jews, it was because they were killing themselves, preferably by gas, and leaving the bills unpaid. I've wondered if this was true—the times gave rise to so many horrors, in the name of senseless pragmatism—or just a joke, a ghastly joke, invented by gloomy candlelight. But whether a bitter joke or reality, no matter: when humor tips into such darkness, it speaks the truth.

In the face of such adversity, things lose their names. They recede from us. And we can no longer speak of suicide. Alma Biro did not commit suicide. Karl Schlesinger did not commit suicide. Leopold Bien did not commit suicide. And neither did Helene

Kuhner. None of them did. Their deaths cannot be linked to their mysterious individual sorrows. We can't even say that they chose to die with dignity. No. They were not ravaged by private despair. Their pain was something collective. And their suicides a crime committed by someone else.

WHO ARE
ALL THOSE PEOPLE?

*S*ometimes a single word is enough to make a sentence take shape, plunge us into reverie. Time is unaffected by this; it carries on, heedless of the surrounding chaos. And so, in the spring of 1944, Gustav Krupp, one of the high priests of industry who, as we saw at the beginning of our story, made his offering to the Nazis and backed the regime from the outset, was dining with his wife, Bertha, and eldest son, Alfried, heir to the *Konzern*. It was their last evening in the Villa Hügel, the vast palace that was their residence and the seat of their power. By now, things had taken a bad turn. Everywhere, German forces were retreating. The Krupps had resigned themselves to giving up their domain and heading for the mountains, far from the Ruhr, to the cold white peace of Blühnbach, where the bombs wouldn't find them.

Suddenly, old Gustav rose from his chair. It had been some time since he'd lapsed into hopeless imbecility. Incontinent and senile, he hadn't said a word in years. But that evening, in the middle of dinner, he suddenly jerked to his feet, hugging his napkin to his chest in a gesture of terror; he pointed a long, bony finger toward the back of the room, just behind his son, and murmured, "But who are all those people?" His wife turned her head, his son looked around. They were very afraid. The corner was submerged in darkness. It was as if the shadows were moving, and silhouettes were crawling in the blackness. But it wasn't ghosts that had frozen his blood, not figments or phantoms, but actual men, with actual faces that stared out at him. He saw enormous eyes, figures appearing from the dark. Strangers. He was terror-stricken. He stood there, petrified. The servants froze. The curtains were like ice. And at that moment, he had the impression of truly *seeing*, as he'd never seen before. And what he saw, what slowly came from the shadows, were tens of thousands of corpses, slave laborers, the ones the SS had supplied for his factories. They emerged from the void.

For years, he had borrowed deportees from Buchenwald, Flossenbürg, Ravensbrück, Sachsenhausen, Auschwitz, and many other camps besides. Their life expectancy was a few months. The prisoners who managed to avoid infectious diseases literally died of starvation. But Krupp wasn't the only one to rent such services. His tablemates from the meeting of February 20, 1933, took equal advantage; behind all the criminal enthusiasm and political posturing, they made out just fine. The war had been profitable. Bayer took on laborers from Mauthausen. BMW hired in Dachau, Papenburg, Sachsenhausen, Natzweiler-Struthof, and Buchenwald. Daimler in Schirmeck. IG Farben recruited in Dora-Mittelbau, Gross-Rosen, Sachsenhausen, Buchenwald, Ravensbrück, and Mauthausen, and operated a large factory inside the camp at Auschwitz, impudently listed as IG Auschwitz on the company's org chart. Agfa recruited in Dachau. Shell in Neuengamme. Schneider in Buchenwald. Telefunken in Gross-Rosen, and Siemens in Buchenwald, Flossenbürg, Neuengamme, Ravensbrück, Sachsenhausen, Gross-Rosen, and Auschwitz. Everyone had jumped at the chance for such cheap

ÉRIC VUILLARD

labor. So it wasn't Gustav who was hallucinating that evening in the middle of a family dinner; it was Bertha and her son who refused to see. For all those dead were indeed there, in the shadows.

Of the six hundred deportees who arrived at the Krupp factories in 1943, only twenty remained a year later. One of Gustav's last official acts, before handing over the reins to his son, was to create Berthawerk, a forced-labor factory named after his wife, which he probably meant as some kind of tribute. The workers there were black with filth, infested with lice, walking three miles in winter as in summer in bare clogs to go from camp to factory and factory to camp. They were rousted awake at four-thirty, flanked by SS guards and trained dogs; they were beaten and tortured. As for supper, it would sometimes last for two hours—not because they were allowed to eat at their leisure, but because they had to wait: there weren't enough bowls to go around.

Now, let us return for a moment to the very beginning of our story and take another look at them, the twenty-four men, all around that table. It seems like any meeting of business leaders. They're wearing the same suits, the same dark or striped ties, the same silk pocket squares, the same gold-rimmed spectacles, the same bald heads, the same reasonable faces as we might see today. The basic style hasn't changed much. Not long after this, in place of their Golden Party Badge, some would proudly wear the Federal Cross of Merit, as a Frenchman might wear the Legion of Honor. The regimes commended them in the same way. Look at them waiting, that February 20, calmly, sagely, while the devil passes right behind them, on tiptoe. They're chatting; their little consistory is just like hundreds of others. Don't believe for a minute that this all belongs to some distant past. These are not antediluvian monsters, creatures who pitifully faded away in the 1950s along with the poverty depicted by Rossellini, or were carted off with the ruins of Berlin. These names still exist. Their fortunes are enormous. Their companies have sometimes merged and formed omnipotent conglomerates. On the website of the ThyssenKrupp group, a world leader in steel, whose headquarters are still in Essen and whose watchwords these days are *openness* and *transparency,* we find a brief note about the Krupp family. Gustav did not actively support Hitler before 1933, we read, but once the latter had been elected chancellor, he demonstrated loyalty to his country. He only became a member of the Nazi Party in 1940, it specifies, upon his seventieth birthday. Deeply committed to the social tradition of the company, Gustav and Bertha never failed, come what may, to visit long-standing employees on the occasion of their golden wedding anniversary. And the biography ends with a touching anecdote: for many years, Bertha devotedly cared for her invalid husband in a small building near their Blühnbach residence. No mention of factories near the concentration camps, or of forced labor, or anything.

During their last meal at the Villa Hügel, once his terror had passed, Gustav quietly took his seat and *the faces returned to the shadows.* They would emerge one more time, in 1958. Jews from Brooklyn demanded restitution. On February 20, 1933, Gustav had unhesitatingly committed astronomical sums to the Nazis, but now his son Alfried was proving less profligate. The man who claimed that the Allies had treated the

Germans "like niggers" would nonetheless become one of the most powerful figures in the Common Market, the king of coal and steel, a pillar of Pax Europaea. Before finally deciding to pay reparations, he made the negotiations drag on for two long years. Every meeting with the attorneys of the *Konzern* was punctuated with anti-Semitic slurs. They nonetheless managed to reach an agreement: Krupp would pay each survivor one thousand two hundred fifty dollars, which as a settlement for all claims was not much. Still, Krupp's gesture was unanimously hailed in the press, and it earned him a gold mine of publicity. Before long, as survivors started coming forward, the amount allocated to each became smaller. They revised it down to seven hundred fifty dollars, then five hundred. Finally, when more deportees filed claims, the *Konzern* notified them that it was unfortunately no longer in a position to honor these voluntary payments: *the Jews had cost too much.*

We never fall twice into the same abyss. But we always fall the same way, in a mixture of ridicule and dread. We so desperately want not to fall that we grapple for a handhold, screaming. With their heels they crush our fingers, with their beaks they smash our teeth and peck out our eyes. The abyss is bordered by tall mansions. And there stands History, a reasonable goddess, a frozen statue in the middle of the town square. Dried bunches of peonies are her annual tribute; her daily gratuity, bread crumbs for the birds.

ÉRIC VUILLARD is a writer and filmmaker born in Lyon in 1968 who has written nine award-winning books, including *Conquistadors* (winner of the 2010 Prix Ignatius J. Reilly), and *La bataille d'Occident* and *Congo* (both of which received the 2012 Prix Franz-Hessel and the 2013 Prix Valery-Larbaud). He won the 2017 Prix Goncourt, France's most prestigious literary prize, for *L'Ordre du Jour*. His most recent book, *Sorrow of the Earth*, was his first published in English; *The Order of the Day* is his second. He lives in Rennes, France.

MARK POLIZZOTTI has translated more than fifty books from the French, including works by Gustave Flaubert, Patrick Modiano, Marguerite Duras, André Breton, and Raymond Roussel. A Chevalier of the Ordre des Arts et des Lettres and the recipient of a 2016 American Academy of Arts & Letters Award for Literature, he is the author of eleven books. He directs the publications program at the Metropolitan Museum of Art in New York.